"I AM"

The Attributes of God Seen in Scripture, Science and Creation

Mario G. DeVita

To Kathy and Dan

With My Love,

Mario

BookLocker
Trenton, Georgia

Print ISBN: 978-1-958890-40-0
Ebook ISBN: 979-8-88531-543-2

Published by BookLocker.com, Inc., Trenton, Georgia, U.S.A.

Printed on acid-free paper.

Library of Congress Cataloguing in Publication Data
DeVita, Mario Gene
"I AM" by Mario G. DeVita
Library of Congress Control Number: 2023912692

BookLocker.com, Inc.
2023

Scripture quotations are from NIV Bible.

DEDICATION

To the man who boldly declared that he was I AM, and
then He proved He was. -- Jesus Christ

TABLE OF CONTENTS

INTRODUCTION 1

CHAPTER 1: GOD IS GOOD 5

CHAPTER 2: GOD IS ALMIGHTY 13

CHAPTER 3: GOD IS MERCIFUL 29

CHAPTER 4: GOD IS SOVERIGEN 41

CHAPTER 5: GOD IS TRIUNE 49

CHAPTER 6: GOD IS HOLY 57

CHAPTER 7: GOD IS JUST 65

CHAPTER 8: GOD IS OMNISCIENCT 73

CHAPTER 9: GOD IS LOVE 81

CHAPTER 10: GOD IS PERSONAL 91

CHAPTER 11 GOD IS ETERNAL 99

CHAPTER 12: GOD IS FAITHFUL 105

CHAPTER 13: GOD IS UNCHANGING 113

CHAPTER 14: GOD IS OMNIPRESENT 121

CHAPTER 15: GOD IS SPIRIT 127

INTRODUCTION

As the saying goes, to know Him is to love Him. But who can truly know God. Can any mortal this side of Heaven know God in His fullness. I think not. However, one can begin with what Scripture says about the attributes of God. That would be a beginning of an attempt to understand the one who is virtually indescribable.

We see in the Bible many of the attributes of God discussed, with several of these given rather extensive coverage. God is: Good, All Powerful, Personal, Sovereign, Holy, Just, Loving, Merciful, Compassionate, all Knowing, Faithful, Unchanging, Eternal and Omnipresent. This book deals with several of these attributes.

A study of the attributes of God in the Bible presupposes a conviction of the Divine inspiration of the scriptures. So, what does the Bible say about itself?

"All Scripture is given by inspiration of God, and is profitable for doctrine, for reproof, for correction, for instruction in righteousness: that the man of God may be perfect, thoroughly furnished unto all good works" (II Tim. 3:16–17). How do we know that the Bible is truly the inspired word of God. The most convincing argument to support that Divine inspiration is fulfilled prophecy. There are hundreds of such prophecies in the Old Testament and a small sample of these deal specifically with Jesus; His lineage (Jeremiah 23:5), the time when He would come into this world (Daniel 2:31-45), the exact town where He would be born (Micah 5:2), some of His titles and power (Isaiah 9:6-7), and many prophecies concerning His character, ministry and death (Isaiah 42-52). Accurate fulfillment of prophecy is a sure sign that a supernatural power is at work.

The most recent example of fulfilled prophecy we have are those given 2500 years in advance in the book of Ezekiel concerning the return of the Jewish people to their homeland. (Ezekiel chapters 35, 36).

In addition to fulfilled prophecy, we have the testimony of many credible witnesses who have no reason to lie or deceive anyone. This is made clear in the beginning of Luke's Gospel (Chapter 1: 1-3) "Many have undertaken to draw up an account of the things that have been fulfilled among us, just as they were handed down to us by those who from the first were eyewitnesses and servants of the word. With this in mind, since I myself have carefully investigated everything from the beginning, I too decided to write an orderly account for you, most excellent Theophilus."

Archeology also substantiates many of the details contained in the Bible. There has not been a single archeological finding that disproves any Biblical details regarding names, places or facts mentioned in either the Old Testament or the New Testament. Further proof of the veracity and Divine inspiration of this unique book.

Logic also dictates that God, with all His wisdom and power, would want to speak in a meaningful and accurate way to the people He created. The Bible does that. Men who were impowered by God's Holy Spirit were chosen to record the history of God's interaction with His people from the very beginning of creation through to the end of this world. And all that was written without error, as only God could do. Not only that, but God also ensured the book preservation, despite its many enemies' continuous attempts to destroy it. It remains the most popular book ever printed.

CHAPTER 1:

GOD IS GOOD

Knowing God must begin with an understanding that we are totally dependent on Him to reveal himself to us. And that is what God did as he inspired men to write, without error, what he decided we needed to know. That written account we have today of course is called the Bible.

The Bible is divided into two parts, the Old Testament and the New Testament. The Old Testament, also known as the Hebrew Bible, was written over a period of approximately 1,000 years, from around 1200 BC to 100 AD. It contains 39 books that were written in Hebrew and Aramaic and covers the history of the Jewish people from the creation of the world to the rebuilding of the Temple in Jerusalem after the Babylonian exile.

The New Testament was written in Greek over a period of approximately 50 years, from around 50 AD to 100 AD. It contains 27 books that describe the life, teachings, death, and resurrection of Jesus Christ, as well as the history of the early Christian Church. It is divided into four main sections: the Gospels, the Acts of the Apostles, the Epistles (or Letters), and the Book of Revelation.

Some of the greatest intellects in history have drawn their inspiration from the Scriptures. Benjamin Franklin said:

"Young man, my advice to you is that you cultivate an acquaintance with and firm belief in the Holy Scriptures, for this is your certain interest." Thomas Jefferson said, "I have said and always will say, that the study of the Sacred book will make better citizens, better fathers, and better husbands."

When the late Queen Victoria was asked the secret of England's greatness, she took down a copy of the Scriptures, and pointing to the Bible she said, "That Book explains the power of Great Britain." Daniel Webster once affirmed, "If we abide by the principles taught in the Bible, our country will go on prospering; but, if we and our posterity neglect its instructions and authority, no man can tell how sudden a catastrophe may overwhelm us and bury all our glory in profound obscurity. How Great is Britain now that so many of their people have all but abandoned the teachings of holy Scripture?

When Sir Walter Scott lay dying, he said, "Read to me out of the Book." Which book? answered his servant. "There is only one Book," was the dying man's response "The Bible!

The goodness of God is a recurring theme throughout the whole Bible, as the authors of the various books repeatedly express their belief in God's benevolent nature and his unfailing love for his people. Throughout the stories and accounts presented in the Old Testament, we see evidence of God's goodness manifested in a variety of ways, from his creation of the world and his providential care for his people, to his grace and forgiveness in the face of human sinfulness and disobedience.

In the opening verses of the book of Genesis, we are introduced to God as the Creator of the universe, who brings order out of chaos and calls all things into being. This act of creation is seen as a profound expression of God's goodness and his desire to share his life with the people He created.

Throughout the Old Testament, we see evidence of God's providential care for his people, as he provides for their needs and protects them from harm. In the book of Exodus, for example, God leads the Israelites out of slavery in Egypt and guides them through the wilderness, providing them with food and water and protecting them from their enemies. The psalmist reflects on this care in Psalm 23, proclaiming: "The Lord is my shepherd, I shall not want. He makes me lie down in green pastures, he leads me beside quiet waters, he restores my soul."

Despite man's disobedience and sinfulness, God repeatedly shows his goodness with grace and forgiveness for his people. In the book of Jonah, for example, God sends the prophet to the city of Nineveh to warn them of their impending destruction. When the people repent of their sins, God relents and shows them mercy, sparing them from the punishment they deserved.

Likewise, the book of Hosea portrays God's steadfast love for his people, even in the face of their unfaithfulness. The prophet marries a prostitute named Gomer, who repeatedly cheats on him and runs away. Despite this, Hosea remains faithful to her and continues to love her, reflecting God's love for his people, who constantly turn away from him.

The book of Isaiah also emphasizes God's grace and forgiveness, as the prophet speaks of a time when God will "take away the disgrace of his people from all the earth and wipe away the tears from all faces and the reproach of his people he will remove from the whole earth." (Isaiah 25:8). This vision of a restored relationship between God and his people is seen as the ultimate expression of God's goodness and mercy.

At the same time, the Old Testament also portrays God as a God of justice, wisdom and righteousness, who expects his people to live according to his standards. The book of Proverbs, for example, presents a vision of the good life that is based on wisdom and righteousness, while warning against the dangers of folly and wickedness.

Similarly, the prophetic books of the Old Testament often denounce injustice and call for the restoration of justice and righteousness. The prophet Amos, for example, speaks out against the oppression of the poor and the abuse of power by the wealthy and powerful, declaring "Hear this you who trample upon the needy and destroy the poor of the land, the Lord has sworn by the pride of Jacob, I will never forget anything they have done." (Amos 8:7).

The book of Job also grapples with the question of God's goodness in the face of human suffering, as Job wrestles with the problem of why bad things happen to good people. In the end, Job comes to a deeper understanding of God's goodness as He restores to Job twice what the devil had taken from him.

The book of Jeremiah says it best, "I know the plans I have for you, declares the Lord, plans to prosper you and not to harm you, plans to give you a hope and a future." (Jeremiah 29: 11). Isn't that what every loving father wants for his children. And so does God.

The New Testament is full of references to the goodness of God, as the authors of the various books repeatedly express their belief in God's benevolent nature and his mercy towards his people. Throughout the stories and teachings presented in the New Testament, we see evidence of God's goodness in a variety of ways, from his loving kindness and care for his creation to his grace and forgiveness in the face of human sinfulness and disobedience.

The gospel of John describes Jesus Christ as the Word of God who was present at the beginning of creation. In John 1:3, we read: "Through him all things were made; without him nothing was made that has been made." This depiction of Jesus as the creator underscores the belief in God's goodness and his desire to share his blessings with his creatures.

Similarly, the apostle Paul speaks of God's providential care for his people in Romans 8:28: "And we know that in all things God works for the good of those who love him, who have been called according to his purpose." This assurance of God's care and concern for his people is seen as an expression of his goodness and his desire to bless them.

One of the central themes of the New Testament is God's grace and forgiveness, which are expressed most fully through the life, death, and resurrection of Jesus Christ. The apostle Paul describes this grace in Ephesians 2:8-9: "For it is by grace you have been saved, through faith—and this is not from yourselves, it is the gift of God—not by works, so that no one can boast." Grace is understood as unmerited favor of God which can neither be earned nor purchased.

This message of grace is also expressed in the parable of the prodigal son, which Jesus tells in Luke 15:11-32. In this story, a wayward son returns to his father's house after squandering his inheritance on wild living. Despite the son's disobedience, the father welcomes him back with open arms and celebrates his return, demonstrating God's willingness to forgive even the most wayward of sinners.

At the same time, the New Testament depicts God's goodness through his justice and righteousness, as the authors of the various books call for God's people to live according to his standards. In Matthew 5:6, for example, Jesus declares: "Blessed are those who hunger and thirst for righteousness, for they will be filled." This hunger for righteousness is seen as a key characteristic of those who seek to follow God's will.

The apostle James calls for a life of active faith that is expressed through deeds of righteousness, as he writes in James 2:17: "In the same way, faith by itself, if it is not accompanied by action, is dead." This call to action underscores the belief in God's goodness and his desire for his people to live just and righteous lives.

God's goodness, love and compassion for his people are expressed most fully through the life and teachings of Jesus Christ. In John 3:16, perhaps the most well-known verse in the Bible, we read: "For God so loved the world that he gave his one and only Son, that whoever believes in him shall not perish but have eternal life." This profound expression of God's love for his creation is seen as the ultimate expression of his goodness.

Jesus demonstrates compassion and love as he heals the sick, feeds the hungry, and welcomes the outcast. In

Matthew 25:40, Jesus declares: "Truly I tell you, whatever you did for one of the least of my brothers, you did unto me."

Perhaps the best expression of the Goodness of God is found in Philippians 2: 6-8 which speaks of the nature of Jesus' sacrifice for the whole world. "Christ Jesus, who, being in very nature God, did not consider equality with God something to be held on to, rather he made himself nothing by taking the very nature of a servant, being made in human likeness. And being found in appearance as a man, he humbled himself by becoming obedient to death— even death on a cross."

One could only imagine the enormity of that transition of Jesus Christ from God to one of His creatures, mankind, knowing beforehand what the cost would be to save those whom He loves so much. Goodness is hardly sufficient a word to describe such an act. It has no equivalent in all human history. However, it might be loosely compared to a man who loves cats so much that he decides to become a member of the feline species to save that species from extinction. In doing so, he would have to restrict himself to the limitations of a cat's ability to function while retaining the memory of all the things he was able to do in his former life as a human being. And after 33 years of sacrificial living, he accomplished his purposes as a cat having saved from extinction those cats who followed him. He then submits to being ruthlessly killed by a pack of angry, jealous cats for no cause.

What kind of a man would do that. The God-Man, Jesus Christ, did something like that, and a whole lot more for us. So Good!

CHAPTER 2:

GOD IS ALMIGHTY

The almighty power of God has been explored in various ways throughout history. The Bible and science (the study of nature) are two areas of study that offer different perspectives on this subject. The Bible provides insight into the nature of God's power through the narratives of creation, the exodus, and other historical events. Science on the other hand, explores the vastness of the universe and the complexity of its systems. By examining both the Bible and nature (science), we can gain a deeper understanding of the power of God, as the evidence for intelligent design is everywhere to be seen.

Perhaps the most profound declaration of God's power in the Bible is found in the book of Isaiah (46: 9-10) "I am God, there is no other. I am God, there is none like me. At the beginning, I foretell the outcome in advance, things not yet done. I say that my plans shall stand, I accomplish my every purpose."

Wow! What more can God say about Himself, and then supports this claim with miracle after miracle beginning with the creation of the world and continuing even to this day with innumerable testimonies of people in all walks of life that were touched by miracles in their own lives. God accomplishes His purposes despite all the evil in this world.

One of the most well-known narratives in the Bible is the story of creation. God created the universe in six days and rested on the seventh day. This conveys the idea that God has the power to create something out of nothing. Science has recently learned that there was a time when the universe as we know it did not exist. But God did, and we call that time eternity past.

The Biblical narrative of creation also highlights the importance of order and structure in the universe. Each day of creation represents a different aspect of the universe, such as light, the sky, the land, and the sea. This structure tells us that God has a purpose for everything in the universe and that everything is interconnected.

Another narrative that illustrates the power of God is the destruction of the world through the great flood. We read the account when God was displeased with the wickedness of humanity and decided to destroy all life on earth with a flood. He instructed Noah to build an ark and to take his family and two of every kind of animal on board. After the flood, God made a covenant with Noah, promising never to destroy the earth with a flood again.

This narrative highlights the power of God to both create and destroy. It also suggests that God is a just God who punishes wickedness and rewards righteousness. The flood represents a kind of cleansing of the Earth, and the power of God to start over and create a new beginning.

The narrative of the exodus is another example of the power of God when He heard the cries of the Israelites who were enslaved in Egypt and decided to rescue them. He sent Moses to lead the Israelites out of Egypt and into the promised land. Along the way, God performed many miracles, including the parting of the Red Sea and the provision of manna and quail in the desert.

This event demonstrated the power of God to intervene in human affairs and to protect his people. It also indicates that God is faithful to his promises and will not abandon his people. The exodus represents a kind of liberation, a way for God to rescue his people from bondage and lead them to freedom.

The conquest of Canaan is another example in the Bible that illustrates the power of God. God commanded the Israelites to conquer the land of Canaan and to destroy its inhabitants. The Israelites were successful in their conquest, and the land became their homeland. This highlights the power of God to give and take away. It also coveys the idea that God has a plan for his people and that he will use his power to help them achieve their goals. The conquest of Canaan was the way for God to bring his people to the promised land and establish them as a nation that would eventually bring forth the Messiah.

In the New Testament we see the life and ministry of Jesus Christ, the central figure and the cornerstone of Christianity. Throughout the Gospels and the rest of the New Testament, we see numerous accounts of the power of Jesus. From healing the sick and feeding the hungry to performing miracles and forgiving sins, Jesus' power is unmatched and undeniable.

In the Gospel of Matthew, we see Jesus begin his public ministry, which is marked by numerous displays of his power. He performs healings, drives out demons, and performs other miracles, such as walking on water and calming a storm.

One of the most significant displays of Jesus' power is his ability to heal the sick. In the Gospel of Matthew, we see Jesus heal a leper (8:1-4), a paralyzed man (9:1-8), a woman with a hemorrhage (9:20-22), two blind men (9:27-31), a mute man (9:32-34), a man with a withered hand (12:9-14), a demon-possessed man (12:22-32), and many others. In the Gospel of John, we see him heal a man who had been paralyzed for 38 years (5:1-15) and a man who was born blind (9:1-12). In each of these cases, Jesus' power is on full display, and those who witness these healings are amazed and convinced of his divinity.

In the Gospel of John, we also see him turn water into wine at a wedding in Cana (2:1-11). In the Gospel of Mark, we see him feed a crowd of 5,000 with just five loaves of bread and two fish (6:30-44). In the Gospel of Matthew, we see him feed a crowd of 4,000 with seven loaves of bread and a few fish (15:32-39). These miracles demonstrate Jesus' power over nature and his ability to provide for the needs of those who follow him.

Another aspect of Jesus' power is his ability to forgive sins. In the Gospel of Mark, we see him forgive the sins of a paralyzed man (2:1-12). This act of forgiveness leads the religious leaders to accuse Jesus of blasphemy, as only God has the power to forgive sins. Jesus responds by healing the man, demonstrating his power and authority to forgive sins. In the Gospel of Luke, we see Jesus forgive the sins of a woman who anoints his feet with oil (7:36-50). This act of forgiveness leads Jesus to declare that her sins are forgiven and that her faith has saved her.

Another manifestation of God's power and sovereignty is seen in the garden when Jesus is arrested by a cohort of Roman soldiers and guards of the chief priests. In John's Gospel (18: 6) when Jesus said the words "I AM" (the very same name God used to identify Himself to Moses) the entire mob retreated and fell to the ground. This was a clear message from God to that mob that He is in control here, and if He should desire, He could have had that mob pinned to the ground and have Jesus walk away free as a bird. But fortunately for us, that was not part of Father's plan for our redemption.

Finally, Jesus' power is on full display in his death and resurrection. In the Gospel of John, we see Jesus willingly lay down his life for his followers (10:17-18). He is then crucified, dies, and is buried. But on the third day, he rises from the dead, as he said He would, demonstrating his power over death (20:1-18). This event is the cornerstone of Christianity, and it is through Jesus' death and resurrection that we are saved. Concerning His death, in John's Gospel (19:30) we see Jesus' last words, "It is finished." Then He bowed His head and delivered up His spirit. It appears that Jesus decided precisely when he would die. He died when His spirit left his body, not by the spear of the Roman soldier.

HE CREATED THE UNIVERSE

Turning now to science (nature) God's power as creator of the universe is clearly established. The universe is vast, complex, and filled with mysteries that have been a source of fascination and inquiry for scientists for centuries. It is estimated that the observable universe, which includes everything that can be seen with modern telescopes, spans about 93 billion light-years in diameter, containing billions of galaxies, each with billions of stars and planets. We know that light-years are a measure of distance, not a measure of time. Scientists tell us the distance in miles of one light year is 5.88 trillion miles. So, the diameter of the observable universe is 93 billion times 5.88 trillion miles. Awesome, what a magnificent manifestation of God's power! The Bible says it this way, "By the word of His mouth the heavens were made."

The complexity of the universe is staggering, and it is reflected in the intricate structures and processes, from subatomic particles to entire galaxies. One of the most striking examples of complexity in the universe is the diversity of celestial bodies that exist. Stars, for instance, come in a wide range of sizes, from tiny red dwarfs that are only a fraction of the size of our sun, to super giants that are thousands of times more massive than our sun. Each type of star has its own unique characteristics, including its lifespan, temperature, and luminosity, and they play a critical role in shaping the evolution of galaxies.

Another aspect of complexity in the universe is the interactions between different celestial bodies. For example, stars can collide and merge, leading to the formation of new, more massive stars. Similarly, galaxies can collide and merge, producing spectacular displays and the formation of new structures.

The complexity of the universe is not limited to the structures and processes that we can observe directly. At the subatomic level, the behavior of particles is governed by the laws of quantum mechanics, which can be difficult to understand. Similarly, the behavior of the universe as a whole is thought to be influenced by mysterious phenomena such as dark matter and dark energy which we cannot see; we can only detect them from their gravitational effects on visible matter.

HE CREATED THE HUMAN BODY

The DNA molecule is the fundamental building block of life on Earth. It contains the genetic information that encodes all the characteristics that make each person unique, from their physical traits to their behavior and personality. The complexity of the DNA molecule arises from its intricate structure and the vast amount of information it encodes, far more than the most complex computer program ever created by man. The DNA molecule contains all the information required to construct every part of the human body.

The human body, made in the image and likeness of God, is a remarkable creation; a complex and intricate system that harbors countless marvels. The brain, as the command center of the body, governs our thoughts, emotions, and actions. The circulatory system, with its intricate network of blood vessels, sustains life by delivering oxygen and nutrients throughout the body. Meanwhile, the skeleton, an architectural wonder, provides structure, protection, and support. By exploring these incredible systems, we gain insight into the awe-inspiring capabilities of the human body.

The human brain is an organ of unparalleled complexity, consisting of billions of neurons and trillions of connections. It is the epicenter of intelligence, consciousness, and memory. Remarkably, this 3-pound organ operates with astonishing efficiency, enabling an array of intricate functions.

The circulatory system, consisting of the heart, blood vessels, and blood, in an intricate network responsible for distributing oxygen, nutrients, hormones, and immune cells throughout the body. The heart acts as a powerful pump, propelling oxygenated blood from the lungs to the rest of the body.

Arteries, the blood vessels branching from the heart, transport oxygen-rich blood to every organ and tissue. Smaller vessels, known as capillaries, facilitate the exchange of oxygen and nutrients with the body's cells. Veins carry deoxygenated blood back to the heart and lungs.

Red blood cells, through their protein called hemoglobin, bind and transport oxygen. White blood cells defend against infections, while platelets promote blood clotting to prevent excessive bleeding. The total length of all blood vessels in the human body is estimated to be around 60,000 miles (96,560 kilometers). This incredible network of blood vessels, if stretched out, could encircle the Earth more than twice.

The skeletal system serves as the structural framework of the human body. It consists of bones, cartilage, and ligaments, working together to provide support, protection, and mobility.

Bones are incredible structures, strong yet lightweight. They come in various shapes and sizes, each with a specific function. Long bones, such as the femur and humerus, enable movement and act as levers. Flat bones, like the skull and sternum, safeguard delicate organs. Irregular bones, such as the vertebrae, provide stability and flexibility. Beyond their mechanical roles, bones serve as reservoirs for minerals.

Now consider one more marvel of God's creative power, the human eye. The human eye is an incredibly complex and sophisticated organ that allows us to perceive the world around us. It is one of the most remarkable systems in the human body, capable of sensing light and producing complex visual images. The complexity of the human eye arises from its intricate structure and the complex neural networks that enable us to see.

The eye is composed of several different structures, including the cornea, iris, lens, retina, and optic nerve. Each of these structures plays a critical role in the process of vision. The cornea and lens focus incoming light onto the retina, which contains specialized cells called photoreceptors that are sensitive to light. The photoreceptors convert the light into electrical signals that are transmitted to the brain via the optic nerve.

HE CREATED THE ANIMAL KINGDOM

We also see in nature another marvel of God's creative power in the animal kingdom, birds, a remarkable species for sure. Birds are one of the most diverse and widespread groups of animals on the planet, with over 10,000 species known to science. They are found in almost every type of habitat, from the icy expanses of the polar regions to the tropical rainforests of the equator.

Birds are characterized by a number of unique physical features that set them apart from other animals. Perhaps the most obvious of these is their feathers, which provide insulation, protection, and the ability to fly. Feathers are arranged in a complex structure that allows for efficient movement through the air. Birds also have a lightweight, but strong skeleton, with many bones fused together to reduce weight and increase rigidity. This allows them to be efficient fliers, even in the face of strong winds and turbulent air currents.

In addition to feathers and a specialized skeleton, birds have a number of other characteristics that help them to survive in their respective environments.

Birds also exhibit a wide range of social behaviors, which can vary greatly depending on the species. Some birds, such as penguins, form large colonies where they live and breed together. Other species, such as eagles, are solitary and territorial, with individuals defending large areas of habitat from intruders. Many species of birds are known for their migratory behavior, where they travel long distances each year to breed or survive in more favorable environments.

HE CREATED SEA CREATURES

Lastly, we examine the most populous creatures God created in this world, the ones we know least about, fish, the inhabitants of the sea,

Fish are aquatic creatures that are found in almost every body of water, from small streams to the vast oceans. The ocean is home to some of the most complex and diverse fish species in the world, with more than 33,000 species identified to date.

Fish are incredibly complex creatures, with a wide range of characteristics that enable them to survive in their respective environments. Many fish species in the ocean are known for their extensive migration patterns. For example, salmon are known to migrate from freshwater streams to the open ocean and back again to spawn. This migration can cover thousands of miles.

Fish use a variety of camouflage techniques to blend in with their surroundings and avoid predators. For example, some fish can change color to match their environment, while others have unique body shapes and markings that make them difficult to spot.

Some fish, such as dolphins and certain species of whales, use echolocation to navigate and locate prey. Echolocation involves emitting high-frequency sounds and listening for the echoes that bounce back.

HE CREATED LAND ANIMALS

Finally, we must mention land animals. Land animals refer to different types of animals that live and thrive on the earth's surface. The diversity of land animals is vast, with millions of species spread across all continents and habitats. This vast number of species of land animals prohibits any detailed description of these creatures in this document, but suffice it to say they are certainly a significant part of God's creation.

Mario G. DeVita

HE CREATED SUPERNATURAL BEINGS

We have examined a relatively small portion of God's creation in the natural world, now let us examine the power of God through his creation of supernatural beings, which we call Angels. Angels are an integral part of God's creation and their power is a topic that is explored throughout the Bible. Angels are described as spiritual beings that serve God and act as his messengers. They are depicted as having great power and are capable of performing supernatural feats. For example, in the Book of 2 Kings 19:35 we read, "That night the angel of the Lord went forth and struct down 185,000 men in the Assyrian camp. Early the next day, there they were, all corpses of the dead."

The Bible describes the origin of angels in the book of Genesis, where it states that God created the heavens and the earth. Angels are described as being present during the creation of the universe and are depicted as heavenly beings. The Bible also suggests that angels were created before the earth was formed, which implies that they are much older than humanity.

In the book of Psalms, the angels are described as being created by God to worship and serve him. The psalmist writes, "Praise him, all his angels; praise him all his heavenly hosts. Praise him, sun and moon; praise him all you shining stars" (Psalm 148:2-3). Angels are also called ministering spirits sent to serve those who are to inherit salvation (Hebrews 1: 14).

In the book of Daniel, the prophet describes a vision he had of an angel who appeared to him. The angel was so powerful that Daniel was unable to stand in its presence.

The prophet writes, "I, Daniel, was the only one who saw the vision; those who were with me did not see it, but such terror overwhelmed them that they fled and hid themselves" (Daniel 10:7).

Angels are described as being able to heal the sick and perform other miraculous deeds at God's direction. In the book of Acts, an angel appears to Peter and tells him to follow him out of prison. Peter follows the angel, and they pass by the guards and prison doors without being noticed. The angel then leads Peter to safety, and he is able to escape (Acts 12:6-11).

Angels are also depicted as having power over the natural world. In the book of Revelation, an angel is described as having the power to control the winds. The angel is instructed to hold back the winds until the servants of God are sealed on their foreheads (Revelation 7:1-3). This passage suggests that angels have the ability to manipulate the natural world to achieve God's purposes.

Having discussed only a sample of God's power exhibited in His creation of the natural and supernatural world, what can we say? What a mighty God we serve! A full revelation of His power and glory is not possible in one lifetime and would likely take an eternity to exhibit. That's what Heaven is for.

So, what about now, do we see God's power operative in the world today? Yes, we do. Any discussion of the power of God would not be complete without mention of the Holy Spirit.

The power of God's Holy Spirit is profound and awe-inspiring, transcending human comprehension. He is the third person of the Holy Trinity, along with God the Father and God the Son (Jesus Christ). The Holy Spirit is often depicted as a divine presence and the source of divine power and guidance.

One of the central roles of the Holy Spirit is to reveal and communicate divine truth. The Spirit inspired the prophets and authors of the Scriptures, guiding them in writing God's Word. Through the Holy Spirit's illumination, believers can gain understanding and wisdom, enabling them to comprehend God's will and purposes. The Spirit convicts' individuals of sin and guides them towards repentance, leading to a transformative relationship with God.

The power of the Holy Spirit is demonstrated in various ways throughout biblical accounts. The Spirit empowers believers, granting them spiritual gifts for the edification of the church and the common good. These gifts include prophecy, healing, miracles, a word of wisdom, a word of knowledge, discernment of spirits, and several others. Through these gifts, the Holy Spirit equips and empowers individuals to serve God and make a positive impact in the world.

Moreover, the Holy Spirit plays a crucial role in the process of salvation. It is the Holy Spirit who regenerates and transforms individuals, bringing them from spiritual death to spiritual life. This is often referred to as being "born again" or experiencing spiritual rebirth. The Holy Spirit indwells believers, becoming a constant presence and guide, offering comfort, strength, and assurance.

Furthermore, the Holy Spirit empowers believers to live a life that reflects the character of Jesus. He produces spiritual fruit, such as love, joy, peace, patience, kindness, goodness, faithfulness, gentleness, and self-control.

Listed here with the Biblical references are some of the things He is doing for the believers.

- In Romans 8:26 Holy Spirit helps us pray and He intercedes for us

- In John 16:13 He guides us into all truth and announces to us things to come.

- In John 14:26 He instructs us in everything and reminds of what Jesus taught us.

- In Revelation 2:7. He speaks to the Church.

- In 1 Corinthians 2:10 He reveals wisdom to us.

- In Acts 9:31 He builds up and consoles the Church.

- In Acts 1:8 and 4:31 He fills us and empowers us by the Baptism in the Holy Spirit.

- In 1 Corinthians 12:8-10 He gives us supernatural gifts.

- In Ephesians 3:16 He strengthens us.

- In 2 Peter 1:21 He Prophesies through us.

- In 1 Thessalonians 1:6 He gives us joy despite great trials.

- In 2 Corinthians 3:17 He gives us freedom.

- In Revelations 22:17 He calls for the return of Jesus.

- In 2 Corinthians 3:18 He transform us into the image of Jesus.

- In 1 Corinthians 3:16 He lives in us making us a temple of God.

- In Romans 8:2 He frees us from the law of sin and death.

- In Galatians 12:8-10 He produces fruit (good character traits) in us.

- In Romans 8:14 He leads us in life.

- In Romans 8:16 He testifies that we are children of God.

- In Ephesians 4:3 He unites us in the Body of Christ.

- In Ephesians 1:13 He seals us as a pledge to our inheritance.

- Matthew 12:28 He enables us to cast our demons.

Is it any wonder that Jesus said to His apostles "It is much better for you that I go. If I fail to go, the Holy Spirit will never come to you, whereas if I go, I will send Him to you." (John 16:7).

CHAPTER 3:

GOD IS MERCIFUL

The mercy of God is a central theme that permeates the scriptures. It is often portrayed through numerous narratives that demonstrate divine compassion and forgiveness. Additionally, throughout history, many individuals have shared remarkable testimonies of experiencing the mercy of God in their lives. The Bible tells us, "Because of the Lord's great love we are not consumed, for his compassions never fail. They are new every morning." (Lamentations 3:22-23). In the book of Micah (6:8) God tells us, among other things, to love mercy. Why is that? Because He loves mercy. Can we see any greater evidence for this than the amazing word Jesus spoke to a criminal being crucified next to Him, "This day you will be with me in paradise."

Any discussion of the mercy of God must include the Bible verse that is so well known, even in our secular culture, "God so loved the world that He gave (sacrificed) His only Son so that whoever believes in Him may not perish but may have eternal life." (John 3: 16). This is of course the epitome of mercy.

When we consider all the works of mercy performed in Jesus' three year public ministry, we would have to remember what the Apostle John wrote at the end of his

Gospel; "If every one of Jesus' works were written down, I suppose that even the whole world would not have room for the books that would be written." (John 21: 25).

One of the earliest instances of God's mercy is seen in the story of Adam and Eve, where despite their disobedience, God shows them mercy by providing clothing to cover their shame and promises them victory over the enemy through the seed of the woman. He could have ended their lives and put an end to all humanity, but he chose mercy and preserved the existence of the human race.

The narrative of Noah and the Great Flood further reveals God's mercy as He spares Noah and his family, once again demonstrating His desire to preserve humanity.

The book of Exodus portrays God's mercy through the liberation of the Israelites from slavery in Egypt. Despite their waywardness and grumbling in the wilderness, God extends His mercy by providing manna, water, fire at night and cloud cover in the day to sustain and guide them. At one point in the wilderness journey God tells Moses, "I see how stiff-necked these people are. Let me alone that my wrath may blaze up against them. Then I will make of you a great nation." But Moses interceded asking the Lord for His mercy on these idol worshippers, and the Lord "repented" in the punishment He had threatened to inflict on His people.

Additionally, the story of the prodigal son illustrates the unconditional love and mercy of God, as the father forgives and embraces his wayward child upon his return.

The Psalms, a collection of songs and prayers, offer expressions of God's mercy. The psalmist repeatedly acknowledges God's mercy as a characteristic of His nature. For instance, Psalm 103 proclaims, "The Lord is compassionate and gracious, slow to anger, abounding in love."

Throughout history, many individuals have witnessed and experienced the mercy of God in their lives. Their testimonies serve as powerful reminders of divine compassion. One such individual is Augustine, a renowned theologian. Augustine's autobiography, "Confessions," recounts his tumultuous youth and eventual conversion to Christianity. He reflects on the mercy of God, acknowledging how God's forgiveness and grace transformed his life.

Another testimony is that of the Apostle Paul, who initially persecuted Christians but later became an ardent follower of Jesus Christ. In his letters, Paul frequently speaks of God's mercy, acknowledging his own unworthiness and the immense grace he received. He declares in 1Timothy 1:13-16, "Even though I was once a blasphemer and a persecutor and a violent man, I was shown mercy because I acted in ignorance and unbelief."

The book of Jonah narrates the story of a reluctant prophet sent to the city of Nineveh to proclaim God's impending judgment. Initially, Jonah attempts to flee from his divine mission but is swallowed by a great fish. In the depths of the sea creature, Jonah repents and cries out to God for mercy. God hears his plea and commands the fish to release Jonah. The prophet then fulfills his duty and delivers the message of impending destruction to the people of Nineveh. Surprisingly, the entire city, from the king to the commoners, responds in repentance, seeking

God's mercy. Witnessing their genuine remorse, God spares Nineveh and demonstrates His boundless mercy.

King David, revered as a man after God's own heart, provides another testament to God's mercy. In the book of 2 Samuel, David's grave transgressions are exposed when he commits adultery with Bathsheba and arranges for the death of her husband Uriah. After being confronted by the prophet Nathan, David acknowledges his sins and pleads for God's forgiveness. In Psalm 51, David pours out his repentance, seeking God's mercy and restoration. Despite the severity of his actions, God responds with mercy, forgiving David and preserving the royal lineage.

The book of Hosea portrays a unique demonstration of God's mercy through the life of the prophet Hosea. God commands Hosea to marry a promiscuous woman named Gomer, symbolizing Israel's unfaithfulness to God. Gomer repeatedly strays from her marriage, engaging in idolatry and immorality. Despite Gomer's unfaithfulness, Hosea remains steadfast in his love and commitment to her, just as God remains faithful to His unfaithful people. In a remarkable act of mercy and grace, Hosea redeems Gomer, paying a price to bring her back into his home. This serves as a powerful example of God's relentless mercy and His willingness to restore His people despite their waywardness.

Among the more contemporary witnesses of God's mercy, we see countless examples of God's mercy manifested in the lives of people we came to know and admire.

Corrie ten Boom, a Dutch Christian who, along with her family, helped hide Jews during World War II. Eventually they were captured and sent to concentration camps.

Despite enduring unspeakable suffering and loss, Corrie ten Boom clung to her faith. In her book, "The Hiding Place," she recounts how, even in the darkest moments, she witnessed the mercy of God sustaining her and providing strength. After her release, she dedicated her life to sharing the message of God's mercy and forgiveness.

Eric Metaxas is a bestselling author and speaker known for his works on faith, history, and culture. He has shared his personal testimony of God's mercy and transformation in his life. Metaxas experienced a period of profound spiritual emptiness and addiction, but through God's mercy, he found redemption and a renewed purpose. His journey has inspired others to seek God's mercy and grace in their own lives, emphasizing the transformative power of a personal encounter with Christ.

John Newton. One of the most well-known stories of divine mercy is that of John Newton, the author of the hymn "Amazing Grace." Newton, a former slave trader, underwent a profound spiritual transformation and dedicated his life to the abolition of slavery. His personal experience of God's mercy inspired the timeless lyrics that have touched countless lives.

Kanye West has expressed a deep sense of receiving God's mercy in his life. He has openly shared his spiritual journey and transformation, which he believes has been guided by God's grace. Kanye has spoken about his past struggles, including mental health issues and personal challenges, and how his faith in God has been instrumental in finding redemption and purpose.

Kanye often speaks about the transformative power of God's mercy in his music and public appearances. He has released albums, such as "Jesus Is King" and "Donda," where he incorporates gospel-inspired lyrics and themes that reflect his spiritual awakening. Through his music, Kanye aims to convey his personal experiences with God's mercy and the profound impact it has had on his life.

Tim Tebow often shares his faith and gratitude for God's mercy and grace in his life. He has spoken about how his faith in God has been a guiding force and a source of strength throughout his career and personal challenges. Tebow frequently emphasizes that his success and achievements are not solely his own doing but a result of God's mercy and blessings.

In interviews and public appearances, Tebow has expressed his belief in God's unconditional love and forgiveness, highlighting that nobody is beyond the reach of God's mercy. He often shares personal stories of redemption, emphasizing how God's mercy has transformed his life and how he strives to extend that mercy and compassion to others.

Lecrae Moore, known professionally as Lecrae, is a Christian hip-hop artist who has gained prominence for his music that combines faith-based lyrics with an engaging rap style. Throughout his career, Lecrae has been open about his personal journey and the ways in which he has experienced God's mercy in his life.

Lecrae's early life was marked by challenges and struggles. He was born in Houston, Texas, and grew up in a broken home. His father left the family when Lecrae was young, leaving him with feelings of abandonment and a void that he tried to fill with various pursuits. As a teenager, Lecrae got involved with drugs, alcohol, and a gang lifestyle.

However, his life took a transformative turn when he encountered the message of the Gospel during his college years. Lecrae began to question the direction of his life and sought a deeper understanding of faith. He eventually became a committed Christian and decided to use his musical talents to express his newfound beliefs.

Lecrae's music reflects his personal experiences, including the struggles he faced and the redemption he found in his faith. He often shares his own stories of brokenness, addiction, and pain, but also emphasizes the hope and mercy he discovered through a relationship with God.

Kathie Lee Gifford, the well-known television host, singer, songwriter, and actress, has publicly shared her faith and belief in God throughout her life. She has spoken about how God's mercy and grace have played a significant role in her personal journey.

One notable aspect of Kathie Lee Gifford's life is her strong Christian faith. She has been open about her spiritual beliefs and has often attributed her successes and triumphs to God's mercy and guidance. Gifford has spoken about the importance of prayer, reading the Bible, and relying on God's strength in times of difficulty.

In the face of personal challenges and tragedies, Kathie Lee Gifford has found solace and strength in her faith. She experienced a profound loss when her husband, Frank Gifford, passed away in 2015. During that time, Gifford leaned on her relationship with God and relied on His mercy to find comfort and healing.

Oprah Winfrey Testifies, "I have always believed in the power of faith, and it was through a difficult period in my life that I truly experienced the mercy of God. There came a time when my career was at a low point, and I felt lost and hopeless. In that moment, I turned to prayer and surrendered my worries to a higher power. To my amazement, doors began to open, opportunities came my way, and I found a renewed sense of purpose. It was as if the universe conspired to help me. I realized that it was God's mercy guiding me through the storm and leading me to a brighter future.

Denzel Washington Testifies, "Throughout my life and career, I have faced numerous challenges and uncertainties. However, one constant has been the mercy of God, which has been a guiding force in my journey. There have been times when I made mistakes, but God's mercy always gave me a second chance. I remember a particular period in my life when I struggled with addiction. It was a dark and difficult time, but through God's mercy, I found the strength to overcome my demons and rebuild my life. His love and forgiveness transformed me from within, and I became a better person. I am humbled and grateful for the boundless mercy that has been bestowed upon me."

Malala Yousafzai Testifies, "As a young girl advocating for girls' education in Pakistan, I faced great adversity and danger. There came a point when I was targeted and brutally attacked by the Taliban. It was during that harrowing experience that I witnessed the mercy of God in its truest form. I miraculously survived the attack, and it was through God's mercy that I was given a second chance at life.

God's mercy gave me the strength to forgive those who harmed me and continue my mission with even greater determination. It is through the mercy of God that I find the courage to face adversity and remain hopeful for a better future for all."

Maya Angelou Testifies, "Throughout my life, I have encountered moments of despair and uncertainty. However, it was during those times that I witnessed the mercy of God, lifting me up and carrying me through the darkest of storms. As a survivor of childhood trauma and discrimination, I found solace in writing and expressing my emotions through poetry. It was through this creative outlet that I experienced the transformative power of God's mercy, healing my wounds and giving me the strength to persevere. God's mercy taught me the importance of forgiveness, both for others and myself."

What can we learn from this last testimony and many more like it? Well, Jesus sums it up very concisely in the Gospel of Matthew (5: 24) "Blest are they that show mercy, mercy shall be theirs." That is a promise from God, and we all need that mercy. Mercy and forgiveness are so closely related as they are virtually identical.

Jesus also spoke to the case when mercy is not shown (Matthew 18: 21-35). Then Peter came to Jesus and asked, "Lord, how many times shall I forgive my brother or sister who sins against me? Up to seven times?" Jesus answered, "I tell you, not seven times, but seventy times seven times. Therefore, the kingdom of heaven is like a king who wanted to settle accounts with his servants. As he began the settlement, a man who owed him ten thousand bags of gold (approximately $3.2 trillion dollars in today's market) was brought to him. Since he was not able to pay, the master ordered that he and his wife and his children and all that he had be sold to repay the debt. At this the servant fell on his knees before him. 'Be patient with me,' he begged, and I will pay back everything. The servant's master took pity on him, canceled the debt and let him go.

But when that servant went out, he found one of his fellow servants who owed him a hundred silver coins. He grabbed him and began to choke him. 'Pay back what you owe me!' he demanded. His fellow servant fell to his knees and begged him, 'Be patient with me, and I will pay it back.' But he refused. Instead, he went off and had the man thrown into prison until he could pay the debt. When the other servants saw what had happened, they were outraged and went and told their master everything that had happened.

Then the master called the servant in. 'You wicked servant,' he said, 'I canceled all that debt of yours because you begged me to. Shouldn't you have had mercy on your fellow servant just as I had on you?' In anger his master handed him over to the jailers to be tortured, until he should pay back all he owed.

This is how my heavenly Father will treat each of you unless you forgive your brother or sister from your heart."

This raises the question; how do we know if we have forgiven our offender(s) from the heart as Jesus said we must? Assuming we have the will to do so, try saying a prayer like this:

"Father God, I choose now to forgive (name) for all he/she has done to hurt me. I forgive (name) fully even as you fully forgave me for all my sins, and I ask you to bless (name) in every way possible. I pray this from my heart, in Jesus' name, Amen. That should work.

Something to consider, if the person you are forgiving is not born again, you would want to ask God to lead him/her to salvation. That would be the very best blessing they could ever receive. You are not responsible for their salvation, that would be the work of the Holy Spirit.

It is worth repeating, God's mercy (forgiveness) is given to those who show mercy (forgiveness) to others.

CHAPTER 4:

GOD IS SOVERIGEN

The sovereignty of God is a fundamental concept in Christianity that asserts the absolute authority, power, and control of God over all creation. It encompasses God's reign and rule over the universe, including His governance of human affairs and His divine will. Throughout the Bible, from the Old Testament to the New Testament, the sovereignty of God is consistently depicted.

The sovereignty of God is evident from the very beginning of the Bible, the book of Genesis. In Genesis 1:1, we read, "In the beginning, God created the heavens and the earth." This verse establishes God as the ultimate Creator and emphasizes His sovereignty over all things. The account of creation demonstrates God's authority to bring forth life, shape the universe, and establish order out of chaos.

Psalm 24:1 affirms, "The earth is the Lord's, and everything in it, the world, and all who live in it." This verse emphasizes the comprehensive ownership and dominion of God over the entire earth. It underscores that everything belongs to God, and He exercises His sovereignty over creation in accordance with His divine purposes.

The sovereignty of God extends beyond creation and encompasses His rule over human history. In the Old

Testament, we encounter numerous instances where God's sovereignty is manifested through His providential guidance and governance.

For example, in the book of Exodus, God reveals His sovereignty in the liberation of the Israelites from Egyptian slavery. Despite Pharaoh's resistance, God displays His power through miraculous signs ultimately leading to the deliverance of His people. Exodus 9:16 declares, "But I have raised you up for this very purpose, that I might show you my power and that my name might be proclaimed in all the earth." This verse highlights God's sovereignty in choosing a particular time and manner for the manifestation of His power, including ten devastating plagues and the death of the first born in every Egyptian household.

Additionally, in the book of Daniel, we witness God's sovereignty over earthly kingdoms and rulers. Daniel interprets King Nebuchadnezzar's dream, revealing that God establishes and removes kings according to His sovereign will (Daniel 2:21). The book of Daniel showcases God's dominion over human affairs and the fulfillment of His divine plan through the rise and fall of empires.

The sovereignty of God also plays a crucial role in the realm of salvation. Ephesians 1:4-5 states, "For he chose us in him before the creation of the world to be holy and blameless in his sight. In love, he predestined us for adoption to sonship through Jesus Christ, in accordance with his pleasure and will." These verses highlight God's sovereignty in the election and predestination of believers. It emphasizes that God's choice to save individuals was made before the foundation of the world, underscoring His supreme authority and foreknowledge. God's foreknowledge of all human history, before man's creation, enabled Him to know how every human being would respond to the Gospel message of salvation. With that unique understanding, God then chooses and predestined them for salvation. We see no mention of any predestinating of lost souls, as scripture tells us, "It is His will that all men be saved and come to the knowledge of the truth about Jesus Christ." (1 Timothy 2: 4). Since God wants all men to be saved, He would be conflicted if He had predestined some to be lost. God is never conflicted.

Romans 8:28 proclaims, "And we know that in all things God works for the good of those who love him, who have been called according to his purpose." This verse indicates that God's sovereignty is intertwined with His providential care and redemptive plan. Even in the midst of challenges and suffering, God is actively working for the ultimate good of His people.

The pinnacle of God's sovereignty is revealed through Jesus Christ, the incarnate Son of God. In the New Testament, Jesus demonstrates His authority and sovereignty over various aspects of life.

In Matthew 28:18, Jesus declares, "All authority in heaven and on earth has been given to me." This statement affirms the extent of Jesus' sovereignty, encompassing both the heavenly realms and the earth. Through His death, resurrection, and ascension, Jesus secures His rightful place as the ruler of all creation.

Furthermore, the book of Revelation portrays Jesus as the triumphant King who will return to establish His eternal kingdom. Revelation 19:16 depicts Jesus with the title "King of Kings and Lord of Lords," emphasizing His absolute sovereignty and dominion over all earthly and heavenly powers.

The sovereignty of God is a pervasive theme throughout the Bible, revealing His supreme authority, power, and control. From the accounts of creation to the narratives of deliverance, from the promises of salvation to the reign of Jesus Christ, God's sovereignty is woven into the fabric of Scripture. It affirms His divine right to rule over all creation.

The Bible is replete with examples that demonstrate the sovereignty of God over all creation. From the Old Testament to the New Testament, we find numerous passages that showcase His supreme authority, providential guidance, and redemptive plan. For example, in:

Job 42:2: "I know that you can do all things; no purpose of yours can be thwarted." This verse from the book of Job affirms God's unlimited power and control. It declares that God's purposes will always prevail, emphasizing His sovereignty even in the face of human suffering and questioning.

Proverbs 16:9: "In their hearts, humans plan their course, but the Lord establishes their steps." This proverb underscores God's sovereignty over human decisions and actions. It highlights that although individuals make plans, it is ultimately God who determines the outcome.

Acts 4:27-28: "Indeed Herod and Pontius Pilate met together with the Gentiles and the people of Israel in this city to conspire against your holy servant Jesus, whom you anointed. They did what your power and will have decided beforehand should happen." These verses refer to the crucifixion of Jesus and highlight God's sovereign plan of salvation. They reveal that even the actions of wicked individuals were within God's foreknowledge and sovereign purpose.

Romans 9:15-16: "For he says to Moses, I will have mercy on whom I have mercy, and I will have compassion on whom I have compassion." It does not, therefore, depend on human desire or effort, but on God's mercy. These verses from Paul's letter to the Romans emphasize God's sovereignty in choosing and showing mercy. They declare that God's selection is not based on human merit but is entirely a result of His sovereign will and His foreknowledge of all human history.

Revelation 4:11: "You are worthy, our Lord and God, to receive glory and honor and power, for you created all things, and by your will, they were created and have their being." This verse from the book of Revelation affirms God's sovereignty as the Creator of all things. It acknowledges that all things exist and have their purpose according to His will, reinforcing His supreme authority.

Isaiah 46:9-10: "I am God, there is no other. I am God, there is none like me. In the beginning I foretell the outcome in advance, things not yet done. I say that my plans shall stand. I accomplish my every purpose."

These are God's own words about His sovereignty spoken to the Prophet Isaiah. It could not be any clearer. "I accomplish my every purpose."

That sounds like the very definition of sovereignty.

John 14: 6 Jesus proclaims the reality of His sovereignty regarding man's salvation in terms that are difficult to misunderstand. "I am the way, the truth, and the life. No one comes to the Father (Heaven) but by me. Notice the words, "the way" not a way; "the truth" not a truth; and "the life" not a life.

These examples, among many others in the Bible, reveal the sovereignty of God over creation, history, salvation, and all aspects of life. They depict God as the supreme ruler.

Recognizing and embracing the sovereignty of God brings comfort, assurance, and reverence. It reminds us that we can trust in His wisdom and goodness, even when circumstances appear uncertain or challenging. The sovereignty of God calls us to submit to His will, align our lives with His purposes, and find peace in His loving rule. Those who do submit to God's sovereignty qualify for His blessings. There are consequences for those who choose not to accept His loving rule over them. In their case the god of this world has blinded the minds of the unbelievers, to keep them from seeing the light of the gospel of the glory of Christ, who is the image of God. (2 Corinthians 4-4). In Luke 19:41, it says, "As Jesus approached Jerusalem and saw the city, he wept over it." due to its rejection of him and the impending destruction that would befall the city. I believe He weeps over every lost soul.

One might ask, if God is both good and sovereign, why does He allow so much evil in this world? This is the question of the ages. Well, we know this much, the greatest evil act perpetrated by mankind in all human history was the crucifixion of their creator, Jesus Christ. We also know this great evil act brought about the greatest good in human history, the opportunity for all men to be saved and live forever with God in unimaginable bliss. So, if God took the greatest evil act in human history and turned it to good, He will do the same for every other evil in this world, at a time of His choosing. How will God do that? I don't know, but He knows.

Let us also keep in mind another word God spoke to the same Prophet, "For my thoughts are not your thoughts, nor are your ways my ways say the Lord. As high as the heavens are above the earth, so high are my ways above your ways and my thoughts above your thoughts." (Isaiah 55:8-9).

CHAPTER 5:

GOD IS TRIUNE

The Trinity is a complex mystery and beyond full comprehension by human intellect alone. Christians believe that God is one being who exists in three eternal persons, and are co-equal. The triune nature of God reflects a profound unity, diversity, and interrelationship within the Godhead. While scriptures provide insight into this doctrine, the Trinity is a matter of faith based on the totality of biblical revelation.

The doctrine of the Trinity emphasizes the unity of God in diversity. The three persons of the Trinity are distinct, yet they share the same divine essence or nature. They are co-eternal, co-equal, and mutually indwelling. This unity in diversity reflects the perfect love and relationship within the Godhead.

Each person of the Trinity has distinct roles and functions, while remaining fully God. God the Father is often portrayed as the central person in the Godhead. Jesus Christ, the Son, is revealed as the incarnation of God, who came to save humanity through his life, death, and resurrection. The Holy Spirit is the one who empowers, guides, and sanctifies believers.

The triune God is characterized by an eternal, loving relationship among the Father, Son, and Holy Spirit. They exist in perfect unity, with each person fully knowing and indwelling the others. Jesus speaks of this unity in John 14:10-11, where he says, "Don't you believe that I am in the Father, and that the Father is in me?... Believe me when I say that I am in the Father and the Father is in me."

Following are some scriptures that are often considered in relation to the Trinity:

Genesis 1: 26 Then God said, "Let us make man in our image, in our likeness ..." God speaking using the plural form of the pronoun (us and our) in referring to Himself.

Matthew 28:19: "Go therefore and make disciples of all nations, baptizing them in the name of the Father and of the Son and of the Holy Spirit." This verse is significant because it combines the three persons of the Trinity in a unified formula for baptism.

2 Corinthians 13:14: "The grace of the Lord Jesus Christ and the love of God and the fellowship of the Holy Spirit be with you all." Here, Paul mentions all three persons of the Trinity, emphasizing their distinct roles and their unity.

John 1:1-14: The prologue of the Gospel of John speaks of the Word (Jesus) being with God and being God from the beginning. It also mentions the role of the Holy Spirit in bringing life and light.

John 14:16-17: "And I will ask the Father, and He will give you another counselor to be with you forever, the Spirit of truth." Jesus promises the coming of the Holy Spirit, referring to Him as the Helper or Advocate, who will be with the disciples forever. In this passage, all three persons of the Trinity are mentioned, with Jesus speaking of His relationship with the Father and the Holy Spirit.

Matthew 3:16-17: At the baptism of Jesus, the Holy Spirit descends on Him like a dove, and a voice from heaven (the Father) declares Jesus as His beloved Son. This event reveals the presence of all three persons of the Trinity simultaneously.

Ephesians 4:4-6: Paul writes about the unity of the Spirit, the Lord (referring to Jesus), and God the Father, highlighting the three persons of the Trinity and their role in the church.

1 Peter 1:2: Peter addresses his letter to the elect, who are "chosen according to the foreknowledge of God the Father, through the sanctifying work of the Spirit, to be obedient to Jesus Christ." This verse mentions the three persons of the Trinity in their distinct roles.

Hebrews 1: 8: But of the Son, the Father says, "Your throne, O God, stands forever and ever."

Acts 2: 33: Jesus, exalted at the right hand of the Father, He first received the Holy Spirit from the Father, then poured out this Spirit out on us.

Ephesians 2: 18: Through Jesus we both have access in one Spirit to the Father.

Analogies are often used to illustrate the concept of the Trinity, although they are imperfect and can never fully capture the divine mystery. Some common analogies include:

Mankind	body, soul, spirit
Family	husband, wife, children
Enemies	world, flesh, devil
Patriarchs	Abraham, Isaac, Jacob
Time	past, present, future
Water	liquid, ice, steam
Matter	height, width, depth
Jesus	priest, prophet, king.
Earth	land, sea, sky
Universe	matter, energy, dark matter.
Tabernacle	Outer court, holy place, holy of holies
Gifts of Spirit	Power gifts, wisdom gifts, spoken gifts
Angels	Archangels, cherubim, seraphim.
Ark of Covenant	10 commandments, Aaron's rod, Manna
Atomic structure	Protons, neutrons, electrons

These triplets may help in grasping the idea of unity in diversity, as they could be a way that God reflects His triune nature. So, are the Trinity's "fingerprints" or "initials" anywhere to be seen? If God had initials, what would it be like? JC for Jesus Christ, not likely it is not inclusive; would it be HS for the Holy Spirit, not likely not likely for the same reason. I suggest His initials, or mark if you prefer, would be the number 3, standing for all the members of the Trinity.

The number 3 biblically represents divine wholeness, completeness and perfection. If there ever was a desire to highlight an idea, thought, event or noteworthy figure in the Bible for their prominence, the number 3 was used to put a divine stamp of completion or fulfillment on the subject.

Do we have any physical evidence of God using the number 3 as His initials? Perhaps we do. Consider the Shroud of Turin, which is believed by many scientists and medical experts to be the true burial cloth of Jesus.

Dr. Robert Bucklin, a renowned pathologist, makes this conclusion after a thorough examination of the shroud, "If I were asked in a court of law to stake my professional reputation on the validity of the Shroud of Turin, I would answer very positively and firmly that it is the burial cloth of Christ."

A new scientific method revealed that the Shroud of Turin may truly originate from the 1st Century, around the time of the death and resurrection of Jesus Christ.

Another scientist who analyzed the Shroud of Turin discovered that it best matched a piece of fabric from the siege of Masada, Israel, in 55-74 AD.

One analysis pointed to factors that could trace the shroud's migration from the Middle East to Europe. That analysis of the shroud showed samples of pollen from the ancient region of Palestine, which could not have developed in Europe.

In the negative picture of the Shroud (page 55) examine the number 3, clearly seen on the forehead. Note that the number is properly oriented on the negative image, the edges of the number 3 point to the left as it should. On the positive photo of the shroud, the number appears backwards, that is the 3 edges on the number point to the right instead of to the left. Amazing! No person attempting a forgery of the cloth in the Middle Ages could have known that since the science of photography wasn't discovered until 1822. Who knew that reversing the orientation of the number 3 on the original cloth and on Christ's body itself would produce a perfect number 3 in the negative view of the Shroud. God knew!

In addition, with the use of the latest technology (spectrochemistry) not a single drop of paint was detected on the entire cloth. This fact was universally accepted. That also destroys the theory that the cloth may have been a forgery. The latest explanation as to how this image was produced postulates that it was created by a sudden burst of radiation. And who knew about radiant energy 1900 years before the birth of the atomic age in the 1940s?

The very existence of the shroud is a miracle, so why not a second miracle, God imprinting his initials (3 for Trinity) on the body to demonstrate all three persons of the Trinity were united in that sacrifice of Jesus. They all experienced the emotional horror of the crucifixion, and all three Divine persons suffered, it wasn't just Jesus; although He did bare the physical pain, the emotional pain was surely felt by both the Father and the Holy Spirit.

There is a well-known song we sing today, "Were you there when they crucified my Lord." The Trinity was there, and they left their mark to prove it.

Negative Image

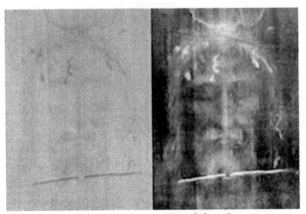

Positive Image   Positive Image

The triune nature of God has profound implications for Christian worship and devotion. Christians address their prayers to the Father, through the Son, in the power of the Holy Spirit. Worship and praise are offered to all three persons of the Trinity, recognizing their distinct roles and acknowledging their unity.

It's important to approach the doctrine of the Trinity with reverence and humility, acknowledging that our human understanding is limited. While the Trinity is a central belief in Christianity, it ultimately points to the mystery and greatness of God, inviting awe and adoration rather than total comprehension.

CHAPTER 6:

GOD IS HOLY

The Bible provides profound insights into the holiness of God. Holiness, in essence, refers to the sacred and transcendent nature of God. It includes His absolute purity, righteousness, and separateness from anything impure or sinful. The Bible describes God's holiness as a defining attribute, setting Him apart from the created world. As it states in Leviticus 19:2, "You shall be holy, for I the Lord your God am holy."

Perhaps the greatest manifestation of God's holiness was seen when Jesus hung on the cross and "God made Him who had no sin to be made sin for us, so that in Him we might become the righteousness of God." (2 Corinthians 5:21). In some mysterious way the sins of this world were laid on Jesus. At that moment, the holiness of God caused the Father to turn away from Jesus, as God's holiness does not allow Him to even look at sin. That is when Jesus cried out "My God, my God, why has thou forsaken me." Immediately afterward He died.

How do we explain the incomparable riches of God's grace. He took our sins and replaced them with His righteousness. Only one way to describe it – Infinite Love. In John 17: 23 Jesus says in His prayer for us to the

Father, "So shall the world know that you love them even as you love me."

Several Bible narratives reveal instances where individuals encountered God's holiness and were overwhelmed by its magnificence. The construction of the Tabernacle and later the Temple served as physical symbols of God's holiness. These sacred spaces were meticulously designed and constructed, signifying the separation between the holy presence of God and the world. God's holiness was so intense that only the high priest, after meticulous preparation and some trepidation, could enter the Most Holy Place only once a year (Leviticus 16:2).

The Torah, the law given to Moses, underscores the holiness of God. Through the commandments, regulations, and ethical teachings, the Israelites were instructed to embody God's holiness in their lives.

Leviticus 11:44 states, "For I am the Lord your God. Consecrate yourselves therefore, and be holy, for I am holy."

God's holiness extends beyond His transcendence; it encompasses His moral purity and righteousness. The prophets, such as Isaiah, Micah, and Amos, emphasize the connection between holiness and justice. Isaiah 5:16 declares, "But the Lord Almighty will be exalted by his justice, and the holy God will be proved holy by his righteous acts."

The Old Testament narratives reveal instances where individuals encountered God's holiness and were overwhelmed by its magnificence. Moses, for instance, witnessed the burning bush and was commanded to remove his sandals for the ground he stood on was holy (Exodus 3:1-6). This encounter highlights the awe-inspiring nature of God's holiness and the reverence it demands. Recognizing God's holiness evokes a sense of reverence and awe. The Psalms repeatedly call for worship and praise, exalting the holiness of God.

Psalms 99:9 proclaims, "Exalt the Lord our God, and worship at his holy mountain; for the Lord our God is holy." God's holiness calls for His people to pursue sanctification and strive for moral purity. Leviticus 20:26 states, "You shall be holy to me, for I the Lord am holy and have separated you from the peoples, that you should be mine."

God's holiness demands a separation from sin and all that is impure.

Habakkuk 1:13 declares, "Your eyes are too pure to look on evil; you cannot tolerate wrongdoing." This highlights the uncompromising nature of God's holiness. God's holiness is not only a call to purity but also

a testament to His mercy and grace. Despite humanity's shortcomings and sinful nature, God extends forgiveness and offers the opportunity for restoration.

Isaiah 6:7 illustrates this beautifully, as the prophet Isaiah, overwhelmed by his own unworthiness in the presence of God's holiness, receives forgiveness: "And he touched my mouth and said: Behold, this has touched your lips; your guilt is taken away, and your sin atoned for." As believers, we are called to reflect God's holiness in our lives.

Leviticus 20:7-8 instructs, "Consecrate yourselves, therefore, and be holy, for I am the Lord your God. Keep my statutes and do them; I am the Lord who sanctifies you." Through obedience to His commands, we strive to mirror God's character of holiness in our thoughts, words, and actions.

In the New Testament, the concept of God's holiness is prominently portrayed through various teachings, interactions, and descriptions. The term "holy" is derived from the Greek word "hagios," which conveys the idea of being set apart, sacred, or morally pure.

The book of Revelation provides a vivid depiction of God's holiness. In Revelation 4:8, the heavenly beings continuously worship God, saying, "Holy, holy, holy, is the Lord God Almighty, who was and is and is to come!" This repetitive declaration emphasizes the divine holiness, underscoring the absolute purity and transcendence of God.

In Matthew 5-7, Jesus delivers the Sermon on the Mount, which outlines the ethical teachings of the Kingdom of God. In Matthew 5:48, Jesus instructs his followers, saying, "You, therefore, must be perfect, as your heavenly Father is perfect." Here, Jesus points to the holiness of God as the standard of perfection to which believers should aspire.

In John 2:13-17, Jesus enters the temple in Jerusalem and drives out the money changers and those selling sacrificial animals. He declares, "Take these things away; do not make my Father's house a house of trade." By cleansing the temple, Jesus displays God's zeal for purity and reverence in worship, demonstrating God's holiness.

The book of Hebrews emphasizes the superiority of Jesus Christ and the new covenant over the old covenant. In

Hebrews 12:14, the author encourages believers, saying, "Strive for peace with everyone, and for the holiness without which no one will see the Lord." This verse emphasizes the essentiality of holiness as a prerequisite for encountering God. Throughout the Bible, believers are urged to pursue holiness as an integral part of their Christian walk.

1 Peter 1:15-16 says, "But as he who called you is holy, you also be holy in all your conduct since it is written, 'You shall be holy, for I am holy.'" This verse emphasizes the call to emulate God's holiness in every aspect of life.

These passages and themes in the Bible highlight God's holiness as an essential attribute. They call believers to strive for holiness, recognizing that God is the standard of purity and moral excellence. Through Christ, believers are empowered to pursue a life characterized by holiness and to reflect the nature of their holy God.

In the account of the Transfiguration found in Matthew 17:1-8, Mark 9:2-8, and Luke 9:28-36, Jesus takes Peter, James, and John up a high mountain. While there, Jesus is transfigured before them, and His face shines like the sun, and His clothes become dazzling white. This event reveals the divine glory and holiness of Jesus, as a voice from heaven declares, "This is my beloved Son, with whom I am well pleased; listen to him!"

In John 17, Jesus prays for Himself, His disciples, and all believers. In verse 11, Jesus addresses the Father, saying, "Holy Father, keep them in your name, which you have given me, that they may be one, even as we are one." Jesus acknowledges the holiness of the Father and seeks His divine protection and unity for His followers. The Holy

Spirit is portrayed as the presence and power of God at work in the lives of believers. His indwelling empowers believers to live holy lives and manifests the holiness of God within them. In 1 Corinthians 6:19-20, Paul reminds believers that their bodies are temples of the Holy Spirit, calling them to glorify God in their bodies.

The Bible also teaches that through the death and resurrection of Jesus Christ, a way was made for humanity to be reconciled with a holy God. In Hebrews 9:12, it states that Jesus "entered once for all into the holy places, not by means of the blood of goats and calves but by means of his own blood, thus securing an eternal redemption." The sacrificial death of Jesus is portrayed as the ultimate expression of God's holiness and love.

In the book of Revelation, the vision of the new heaven and new earth is presented, where God's holiness is fully realized and experienced. Revelation 21:27 states, "But nothing unclean will ever enter it, nor anyone who does what is detestable or false, but only those who are written in the Lamb's book of life." The ultimate consummation of God's holiness is depicted in the eternal dwelling place of His people, free from sin and corruption. This we know was made possible by God's grace and not by any good works we achieved in this lifetime.

In Ephesians 2: 4-9 "But because of His great love for us, God who is rich in mercy, made us alive with Christ even when we were dead in transgressions – it is by grace you have been saved. And God raised us up with Christ and seated us with Him in the heavenly realms in Christ Jesus in order that in the coming ages He might show the incomparable riches of His grace expressed in His kindness to us in Christ Jesus. For it is by grace you have been saved through faith and this is not from yourselves, it is the gift of God, so that no one can boast.

So, how then does God see the Church, the Bride of Christ. There are several passages in the Bible that convey the idea of how God sees His church as spotless and guiltless. These verses emphasize the redemptive work of Jesus Christ and the transformative power of His sacrifice.

Ephesians 5:25-27. "Husbands, love your wives, just as Christ loved the church and gave himself up for her to make her holy, cleansing her by the washing with water through the word, and to present her to himself as a radiant church, without stain or wrinkle or any other blemish, but holy and blameless." This verse portrays Christ's love for the church as sacrificial, comparing it to a husband's love for his wife. It speaks of Jesus' work of purification and sanctification, cleansing the church from sin and presenting her as a holy and blameless entity.

Colossians 1:21-22. "Once you were alienated from God and were enemies in your minds because of your evil behavior. But now He has reconciled you by Christ's physical body through death to present you holy in his sight, without blemish and free from accusation." This passage highlights the reconciling power of Jesus' death, proclaiming that believers are made holy in God's sight. Through Christ's sacrifice, they are presented as faultless and free from accusation, despite their previous state of separation and enmity.

Corinthians 5:17. "Therefore, if anyone is in Christ, the new creation has come; the old has gone, the new is here!" This verse speaks to the transformative nature of salvation. Through faith in Christ, believers become new creations, liberated from the bondage of sin and its guilt. In God's eyes, they are seen as entirely new beings, unblemished by their past transgressions.

These scriptures affirm that God, through the redeeming work of Jesus Christ, sees His church as spotless, blameless, and free from guilt. They emphasize the sanctifying power of God's love and the transformative impact of salvation on believers. We are perceived as having the righteousness of God in Christ. Wow, does it get any better than that? We are so blessed. It is worth repeating, this exalted state of righteousness is not something we earn, but is a gift from God to His children He loves so much.

CHAPTER 7:

GOD IS JUST

The concept of God's justice is a complex and multifaceted one. In the Bible, God is often depicted as a righteous and just deity who rewards the righteous and punishes the guilty. In the Old Testament, God establishes a moral law and gives commandments to the Israelites. These laws provide a framework for justice and righteousness, and those who follow them are considered just in the eyes of God. God expects people to obey His commandments and live according to His standards of righteousness.

The crucifixion of Jesus Christ exemplifies the pinnacle of God's justice. It demonstrates God's holiness, His judgment upon sin, and His mercy extended to humanity through the sacrificial death of Jesus. All sin is considered a crime against God, and true justice demands punishment for all crimes. Even our own system of justice, imperfect as it is, strives to achieve this end. The severity of the punishment is a function of the injury and the dignity of the offended party. A crime (sin) against an eternal, righteous, holy being, and creator of all things would necessarily deserve capital punishment, a death sentence. Jesus Christ took that punishment for us, thus satisfying God's perfect justice. An eternal being paid the price that finite beings could never pay. One of the last words Jesus spoke from the cross, "Tetelestai" in the original language, is translated as "Paid in full."

God's justice is often seen in the form of retribution, where individuals or nations face consequences for their actions. For example, the story of the Israelites' exodus from Egypt shows God's justice in the plagues that befell the Egyptians for their mistreatment of the Israelites. Exodus 12: 36 gives more light on God's justice, "The Lord made the Egyptians favorably disposed toward the people, and gave them whatever they asked for, so they plundered the Egyptians."

God's justice is also closely tied to the concept of covenant in the Old Testament. God entered into a covenant with the people of Israel, promising blessings for obedience and curses for disobedience. This covenantal justice means that God holds His people accountable for their actions and ensures that justice is upheld within the covenant relationship. (Deuteronomy 11: 26-28).

While God's justice often involves punishment for wrongdoing, there is also a theme of restorative justice. God's desire is not solely to punish but also to restore and reconcile. The prophetic books frequently speak of God's desire to bring healing, forgiveness, and reconciliation to those who turn back to Him.

Throughout the Old Testament, God's justice extends beyond individual actions to encompass societal and communal matters. God is portrayed as caring for the oppressed, the marginalized, and the vulnerable, and He expects His people to do the same. The prophets frequently speak out against social injustices, such as mistreatment of the poor, widows, orphans, and foreigners, and call for justice and righteousness in society.

It is important to note that the Bible presents a range of perspectives and images of God's justice, and these perspectives can sometimes seem contradictory. However, when considering the justice of God, it is helpful to understand these various aspects and how they contribute to the overall understanding of God's character and His relationship with humanity.

Alongside God's justice, we also see His mercy and compassion. While God punishes the wicked, He is also portrayed as a God who shows compassion and offers forgiveness to those who repent. The story of Jonah and the city of Nineveh serves as an example of God's willingness to extend mercy even to those who have acted unjustly.

The prophets played a crucial role in calling out injustice and urging the people to pursue justice. They challenged oppressive rulers, criticized corrupt systems, and called for the fair treatment of all individuals. The prophetic writings highlight God's desire for justice to be established in human affairs and for His people to act justly.

The Old Testament also presents the concept of redemption and atonement as a means of restoring justice. Sacrificial rituals and the Day of Atonement (Yom Kippur) were significant elements of Israel's religious practices. These rituals symbolized the people's acknowledgment of their sins, seeking forgiveness from God, and the restoration of a right relationship with Him.

God's justice is often associated with divine judgment and vindication. The belief was that God would ultimately bring judgment upon the wicked and vindicate the righteous. This idea is seen in the Psalms, where the psalmist often calls upon God to intervene and bring justice to those who are oppressed.

The Bible portrays God's justice as operating not only in the immediate present but also with a long-term perspective. Sometimes the full consequences of one's actions are not immediately apparent, and God's justice is understood to be unfolding over time. This perspective emphasizes the importance of trust and faithfulness to God's principles, even in the face of apparent injustice.

The Bible reveals profound insights into the nature of God and His justice. God's justice, as portrayed in the New Testament, encompasses His fairness, righteousness, and the fulfillment of His divine plan. It emphasizes God's attributes of love, mercy, and holiness as integral components of His justice. The interplay between these attributes forms the foundation of God's justice.

God's justice is intertwined with His redemptive plan for humanity. The atoning sacrifice of Jesus Christ, His resurrection, and the offer of salvation to all reflect God's justice, aiming to restore a broken relationship between humanity and Himself.

Jesus' teachings in the Sermon on the Mount, particularly the Beatitudes, convey a radical understanding of justice. He highlights the reversal of societal norms, mercy toward others, forgiveness, and a call for righteousness. He employed parables to illustrate God's justice. Parables like the Prodigal Son, the Good Samaritan, and the Workers in the Vineyard reveal God's willingness to forgive, His impartiality, and the inclusiveness of His justice.

God's justice is inseparable from the offer of salvation. Through faith in Jesus Christ, God's justice is displayed by pardoning the sins of believers and granting them eternal life. The writings of the Apostle Paul expound on God's justice within the context of justification by faith. Paul emphasizes the righteousness imputed to believers through Christ and the harmonization of justice and mercy in God's plan of salvation. The apostolic writings also address the practical implications of God's justice. They call believers to imitate God's justice by pursuing righteousness, promoting social justice, and loving others.

The Bible affirms the ultimate fulfillment of God's justice in the final judgment. The judgment will ensure that all individuals are held accountable for their actions and decisions, rewarding the righteous and administering justice to the unrighteous.

God's justice necessitates the existence of eternal consequences for individuals' choices. The Bible describes the concepts of heaven and hell, underscoring God's justice in the eternal destinies of individuals based on their response to His redemptive plan.

The New Testament presents a comprehensive picture of God's justice, revealing its various dimensions and implications. From the teachings of Jesus to the apostolic writings, the authors portray a God who is both just and merciful. The following verses provide further insight into God's justice underscoring the accountability, judgment, and consequences that await individuals based on their actions and choices.

Romans 2:6-8. "God will repay each person according to what they have done. To those who by persistence in doing good seek glory, honor and immortality, he will give eternal life. But for those who are self-seeking and who reject the truth and follow evil, there will be wrath and anger."

Thessalonians 1:6-7. "God is just: He will pay back trouble to those who trouble you and give relief to you who are troubled, and to us as well. This will happen when the Lord Jesus is revealed from heaven in blazing fire with his powerful angels."

Revelation 19:1-2. "After this I heard what sounded like the roar of a great multitude in heaven shouting: Hallelujah! Salvation and glory and power belong to our God, for true and just are his judgments."

Revelation 20:12-13. "And I saw the dead, great and small, standing before the throne, and books were opened. Another book was opened, which is the book of life. The dead were judged according to what they had done as recorded in the books. The sea gave up the dead that were in it, and death and Hades gave up the dead that were in them, and each person was judged according to what they had done."

Matthew 25:31-46. "When the Son of Man comes in his glory, and all the angels with him, he will sit on his glorious throne. All the nations will be gathered before him, and he will separate the people one from another as a shepherd separates the sheep from the goats. He will put the sheep on his right and the goats on his left... Then they will go away to eternal punishment, but the righteous to eternal life."

Luke 12:2-3. "There is nothing concealed that will not be disclosed or hidden that will not be made known. What you have said in the dark will be heard in the daylight, and what you have whispered in the ear in the inner rooms will be proclaimed from the roofs."

CHAPTER 8:

GOD IS OMNISCIENCT

Scripture reveals that God is indeed omniscient, meaning He possesses complete and perfect knowledge of all things. This attribute of God is often emphasized throughout various religious texts and is an essential aspect of His nature.

One of the key verses that speaks about God's omniscience is found in the book of Psalms: "Great is our Lord and mighty in power; his understanding has no limit." (Psalm 147:5). This verse highlights God's boundless understanding, indicating that there is no limit to His knowledge.

Isaiah 46:9-10. Declares: "Remember the former things, those of long ago; I am God, and there is no other; I am God, and there is none like me. I make known the end from the beginning, from ancient times, what is still to come. I say, 'My purpose will stand, and I will do all that I please." This passage emphasizes that God not only knows the present but also has knowledge of the past and future. He has a comprehensive understanding of all things, including events that are yet to occur. There is no one like Him.

When it comes to personal testimonies, individuals often share experiences where they feel a deep sense of God's omniscience in their lives. These testimonies can vary widely, but they all reflect the supernatural wisdom of God, and His willingness to respond to our needs.

Divine Guidance

Many people testify to moments when they have sought God's wisdom and guidance in making important decisions. They recount instances where, through prayer or reflection, they have felt a profound clarity or received specific insights that seemed to come from a higher source. These moments often reveal God's omniscience as He imparts knowledge and understanding beyond human capabilities.

Answered Prayers

People frequently share stories of how their prayers were answered in unexpected ways. They may have prayed for a solution to a problem or for guidance in a particular situation, and God's omniscience is evident when the answer provided is precisely what was needed, even if it wasn't what was initially anticipated.

Several personal testimonies provide glimpses of how individuals have experienced God's omniscience in their lives. It's important to note that these personal accounts are not uncommon in the lives of believers. While they offer glimpses into the personal experiences of individuals, they may not serve as universal proof of God's omniscience. Ultimately, belief in God's omniscience is often rooted in faith and a broader understanding of scripture.

Bethany Hamilton is a professional surfer who lost her left arm in a shark attack when she was 13 years old. She prayed for the strength to continue pursuing her passion for surfing, and God answered her prayers by enabling her to not only surf again but also compete professionally and inspire others with her story.

Ravi Zacharias was a renowned Christian apologist and speaker. He shares how he prayed for opportunities to reach intellectuals and skeptics with the message of Christ. God answered his prayers by opening doors for him to engage with leading thinkers, philosophers, and academics, ultimately impacting countless lives through his ministry.

Joni Erickson Tada is an author, speaker, and advocate for people with disabilities. After a diving accident that left her paralyzed from the neck down, she prayed for God's help and healing. Though physical healing did not come, God faithfully answered her prayers by giving her strength, purpose, and a platform to inspire others through her ministry and writings.

Eric Liddell was an Olympic athlete portrayed in the movie "Chariots of Fire." He prayed for God's guidance and strength to compete in the 1924 Olympics. Despite facing various obstacles, God answered his prayers by granting him victory and the opportunity to glorify God through his athletic achievements.

Corrie ten Boom was a Dutch Christian who helped many Jews escape the Holocaust during World War II. She shares how she and her family prayed for protection and wisdom as they risked their lives to save others. Despite being arrested and sent to concentration camps, God remained faithful by sustaining them and using their lives to bring hope and comfort to countless prisoners.

George Müller was a Christian evangelist and founder of orphanages in 19th-century England. He relied solely on prayer and God's provision to meet the needs of thousands of orphaned children under his care. Müller often prayed for specific needs, and time and again, God answered his prayers by providing food, clothing, and finances at the exact moment they were required, demonstrating His faithfulness and love.

Jackie Pullinger is a British missionary who has dedicated her life to helping drug addicts and prostitutes in the infamous Walled City of Hong Kong. She prayed for God's guidance and wisdom as she stepped into this challenging environment. God faithfully answered her prayers by transforming countless lives, bringing hope and deliverance to those trapped in addiction and despair.

Louis Zamperini was an American Olympic athlete and World War II prisoner of war. While stranded at sea and enduring brutal conditions in a Japanese prison camp, Zamperini fervently prayed for deliverance and survival. God answered his prayers by miraculously protecting him, providing him with strength and endurance, and ultimately leading him to forgiveness and redemption.

Lecrae is a Grammy-winning Christian hip-hop artist and author known for his transparent lyrics and testimony. He prayed for God to use his music to impact lives and bring hope to those who are hurting. God faithfully answered his prayers by opening doors for his music to reach millions, allowing Lecrae to share his own story of transformation and inspire others with the message of God's love and grace.

Some individuals report experiences where they feel a direct connection to God, during which they receive insights or revelations that were previously unknown to them. These experiences often reinforce the belief in God's omniscience as He imparts knowledge that surpasses human comprehension.

Divine Intervention

Many people share stories of unexpected interventions in their lives that they attribute to God's omniscient knowledge. They may recount moments where they narrowly avoided a dangerous situation or received timely help that they believe was orchestrated by God. These experiences serve as powerful reminders of His all-knowing nature.

Prophetic Revelations

Throughout history, individuals received prophetic messages from God, wherein they receive knowledge of future events or insights into unknown circumstances. These revelations, when accurately fulfilled, provide a tangible demonstration of God's omniscience. This was especially true in the lives of the Prophets in the Old Testament including: Abraham, Moses, Daniel, Samuel, Joseph, Isaiah, Jeremiah, Ezekiel, Zechariah and others.

Comfort in Times of Need

Testimonies often include instances where individuals find solace in God's omniscience during times of sorrow, grief, or uncertainty. They describe moments when they felt a profound sense of God's presence and His deep understanding of their pain and struggles. This awareness brings them comfort and reassurance that they are not alone. The Psalms of David are prime examples of such.

Detailed Guidance

Some testimonies involve accounts of individuals receiving precise guidance or instructions from God in navigating complex situations. They recall moments when they had to make critical decisions, and through prayer and seeking God's wisdom, they received specific guidance that brought clarity and ultimately led to positive outcomes. There are many other scriptures that attest to God's omniscience. For example:

Psalm 139: 1-3. "O Lord, you have searched me and you know me. You know when I sit and when I rise; you perceive my thoughts from afar. You discern my going out and my lying down; you are familiar with all my ways." This Psalm of David emphasizes God's intimate knowledge of every individual. He knows our thoughts, actions, and even our daily routines. It reveals His all-encompassing awareness and understanding.

Psalm 139: 4. "Before a word is on my tongue you, Lord, know it completely." This verse reveals that God knows our words even before they are spoken. His knowledge extends beyond our external actions, delving into the depths of our hearts and minds. Amazing!

Job 34: 21. "For his eyes are on the ways of mortals; he sees their every step." In the book of Job, it is affirmed that God's gaze is continuously upon humanity. He observes and knows every step we take, further highlighting His omniscient nature.

Romans 11:33. "Oh, the depth of the riches and wisdom and knowledge of God! How unsearchable are his judgments and how inscrutable his ways!"

Hebrews 4:13. "And no creature is hidden from his sight, but all are naked and exposed to the eyes of him to whom we must give account."

1 John 3:20. "For whenever our heart condemns us, God is greater than our heart, and he knows everything."

Matthew 10:29-30. "Are not two sparrows sold for a penny? And not one of them will fall to the ground apart from your Father. But even the hairs of your head are all numbered."

1 Corinthians 2:10-11. "These things God has revealed to us through the Spirit. For the Spirit searches everything, even the depths of God. For who knows a person's thoughts except the spirit of that person, which is in him? So also no one comprehends the thoughts of God except the Spirit of God.

Perhaps the best way to understand this concept of God's omniscience is by meditating on this truth, "God knows everything about everything, and everything about everyone." The following scripture verse testifies to this amazing truth.

Ephesians 1: 3-6. Blessed be the God and Father of our Lord Jesus Christ, who has blessed us with every spiritual blessing in the heavenly places in Christ, just as He chose us in Him before the foundation of the world that we should be holy and without blame before Him in love, having predestined us to adoption as sons by Jesus Christ to Himself, according to the good pleasure of His will, to the praise of the glory of His grace, by which He made us accepted in the Beloved.

One must wonder what criteria God uses in making these choices regarding "adoption as sons" or in other words, one's salvation. God being a rational being must surely have some reason for choosing us as His children. Hebrews 11: 6 gives us some insight into this all-important question, "God is a rewarder of those who diligently seek Him." With His foreknowledge of all human history, He knew how each person would respond to the Gospel message before they were born. The reward He gives to those who diligently seek Him with their whole heart is a revelation of the truth of who Jesus Christ is and the grace to accept Him as their Lord and savior. That is the only reward that is meaningful in this life and worthy to be called a promise from God.

CHAPTER 9:

GOD IS LOVE

The Bible states in 1 John 4:16, "God is love." This passage does not say that God is Loving, although He certainly is loving, but it says that the very nature of God is love. That is His essence. Another way of seeing this truth is to understand that everything God does and everything God chooses not to do, is motivated by love. We can speak loosely and say that God seems to have a one-track mind; may be so, and that one track is the love track. Love is called one of the fruits of the Spirit, but it is not the only one.

The fruit of the Spirit are outlined in the Bible and include love, joy, peace, patience, kindness, goodness, faithfulness, gentleness, and self-control. These qualities of the Holy Spirit are shared with the Father and the Son, as they are totally united in mind, will, and purposes. Each fruit represents a specific virtue or characteristic that reflects the nature of God and is intended to be cultivated in the lives of His followers. In the Bible, God demonstrated these qualities through various events and interactions with His people. Following are descriptions of each fruit and how God exemplified them:

LOVE

Love is the foundational fruit of the Spirit. God's love is unconditional and sacrificial. In the Bible we see that God demonstrated His love by choosing and redeeming the nation of Israel as His people, despite their repeated disobedience and unfaithfulness. God's love is exemplified throughout the Old Testament in His covenant relationship with Israel. His love is demonstrated in choosing Abraham and his descendants, delivering them from slavery in Egypt, and providing for them in the wilderness despite their disobedience (Deuteronomy 7:7-9).

Jesus demonstrated love throughout His ministry, particularly through His selfless actions. One prominent example is found in John 15:13, where Jesus says, "Greater love has no one than this: to lay down one's life for one's friends." This verse illustrates His ultimate act of love when He willingly sacrificed Himself on the cross for the salvation of humanity. Jesus demonstrated love when He forgave and restored Peter after Peter denied Him three times. In John 21:15-17, Jesus asked Peter three times if he loved Him and then instructed him to feed and care for His sheep, symbolizing His forgiveness and restoration of Peter's relationship with Him.

JOY

Joy is an inner delight and satisfaction that comes from knowing and experiencing God's presence. God's joy was evident when the Israelites returned from exile and rebuilt the temple, as described in the book of Ezra. God's delight was also seen in the celebrations of feasts and festivals that

He commanded His people to observe. God's joy is evident in the rejoicing and celebrations He commanded His people to observe, such as the feasts of Passover and Tabernacles (Deuteronomy 16:14-15). The book of Zephaniah also describes God's rejoicing over His people with singing (Zephaniah 3:17).

Although Jesus faced various challenges, He exhibited joy in His relationship with God and in His mission. In John 15:11, Jesus says, "I have told you this so that my joy may be in you and that your joy may be complete." His joy stemmed from His obedience to God and His desire for others to experience that same joy. Jesus displayed joy when He rejoiced in the Holy Spirit during His ministry. In Luke 10:21, Jesus, full of joy through the Holy Spirit said, "I praise you, Father, Lord of heaven and earth, because you have hidden these things from the wise and learned and revealed them to little children.'"

PEACE

Peace is the state of tranquility and harmony that comes from being in a right relationship with God. God demonstrated His peace by providing protection and deliverance to His people, such as when He parted the Red Sea and led the Israelites out of Egypt, bringing them from a state of bondage to freedom. God's peace is seen in His provision and protection for His people. One example is when He assured Joshua of His presence and promised to give him peace as he led the Israelites into the Promised Land (Joshua 1:9). Jesus consistently brought peace, both in His teachings and in His interactions with others. In John 14:27, Jesus says, "Peace I leave with you; my peace

I give you. I do not give to you as the world gives. Do not let your hearts be troubled and do not be afraid." Jesus offered a peace that surpassed worldly understanding and provided comfort and assurance to His followers. Jesus exhibited peace when He calmed the storm on the Sea of Galilee. In Mark 4:39, Jesus stood up, rebuked the wind, and said to the waves, "Quiet! Be still!" The wind ceased, and there was a great calm, demonstrating His authority over the forces of nature and bringing peace to His disciples.

PATIENCE

Patience is the ability to endure and wait without losing faith or becoming frustrated. God demonstrated His patience toward the Israelites during their wilderness journey, even though they complained, rebelled, and doubted His provision. He continued to guide and provide for them. God's patience is demonstrated throughout the Old Testament, particularly in His dealings with the Israelites during their wanderings in the wilderness. Despite their grumbling and rebellion, God showed patience and mercy by not destroying them (Exodus 34:6-7).

Jesus displayed patience when He interacted with the Samaritan woman at the well. In John 4:16-18, Jesus engaged in a conversation with her, patiently addressing her questions and helping her recognize her need for living water, even though she initially struggled to grasp His message. Jesus demonstrated patience through His interactions with His disciples and others who lacked understanding or faith. In Luke 9:41, when the disciples struggled to heal a boy, Jesus replied, "You unbelieving and perverse generation, how long shall I stay with you and put up with you?" Despite their shortcomings, Jesus remained patient with them and continued to teach and guide them.

KINDNESS

Kindness involves showing compassion and consideration towards others. In the Old Testament, God displayed His kindness by rescuing His people from their enemies, providing for their needs, and forgiving their sins. One example is when He spared the city of Nineveh after they repented, showing mercy and kindness to the people. God's kindness is evident in His acts of compassion and mercy towards His people. For instance, when the Israelites were hungry in the wilderness, God provided manna for them to eat (Exodus 16:4) and quenched their thirst by bringing water from a rock (Exodus 17:6).

Jesus consistently showed kindness and compassion towards people, especially those who were marginalized or in need. In Matthew 14:14, it is written, "When Jesus landed and saw a large crowd, he had compassion on them and healed their sick." His acts of kindness extended to physical healing, emotional support, and teaching the truth. Jesus showed kindness when He healed the leper who approached Him for help. In Mark 1:40-42, Jesus was moved with compassion and stretched out His hand, touching the leper and saying, "I am willing. Be clean!" His act of kindness not only healed the leper physically but also restored his dignity and social acceptance.

GOODNESS

Goodness refers to moral excellence and doing what is right. God's goodness is evident throughout the Old Testament as He consistently demonstrated His faithfulness, righteousness, and justice. His provision of the Ten Commandments and His laws were expressions of His goodness, guiding His people in righteous living. God's goodness is displayed in His righteous and just actions. One example is when He rescued His people from slavery in Egypt, delivering them with signs and wonders (Exodus 15:11). His provision of the Law and commandments also reveals His desire for their good (Psalm 119:68).

Jesus exemplified goodness in all aspects of His life, always doing what was right and pleasing to God. In Acts 10:38, it is described, "God anointed Jesus of Nazareth with the Holy Spirit and power, and he went around doing good and healing all who were under the power of the devil because God was with him." Jesus' actions consistently reflected the goodness of God. Jesus exemplified goodness when He defended the woman caught in adultery. In John 8:10-11, Jesus challenged her accusers by saying, "If any one of you is without sin, let him be the first to throw a stone at her." His act of goodness protected her from condemnation and offered her a chance for repentance and transformation.

FAITHFULNESS

Faithfulness is the quality of being reliable and trustworthy. God exhibited His faithfulness by keeping His promises to the patriarchs, such as Abraham, Isaac, and Jacob. He remained true to His covenant, even when His people were unfaithful, demonstrating His steadfastness and loyalty. God's faithfulness is highlighted throughout the Bible, even when His people were unfaithful. Despite their idolatry and disobedience, God remained true to His covenant promises and continued to guide and protect them (Psalm 36:5). Jesus displayed unwavering faithfulness to God's will and His mission. In Hebrews 3:2, Jesus is described as "faithful to the one who appointed him." Throughout His ministry, Jesus trusted in God's plan and faithfully carried out His Father's work, even when faced with great challenges and temptations. Jesus displayed faithfulness when He endured the agony of the crucifixion, remaining committed to God's plan for the redemption of humanity. In Luke 23:46, as Jesus breathed His last, He cried out, "Father, into your hands, I commit my spirit!" His unwavering faithfulness in fulfilling God's purpose brought salvation to all who believe in Him.

GENTLENESS

Gentleness involves humility, meekness, and showing kindness towards others. God exhibited gentleness by comforting His people, especially during times of distress. He demonstrated compassion and understanding when they were in need and provided them with reassurance and hope. God's gentleness is demonstrated in His compassionate care for His people. He is described as a gentle shepherd who leads His flock with care and tenderness (Isaiah 40:11). He also comforts and consoles His people in times of distress (Isaiah 49:13).

Jesus exhibited gentleness and tenderness, especially towards those who were broken and repentant. In Matthew

11:29, Jesus says, "Take my yoke upon you and learn from me, for I am gentle and humble in heart, and you will find rest for your souls." His gentle nature drew people to Him and provided solace for those burdened by sin and suffering. Jesus exhibited gentleness when He interacted with children. In Mark 10:13-16, Jesus welcomed the little children who were brought to Him, embracing them and blessing them. His gentleness and affection for children demonstrated His care for the vulnerable and highlighted the value He placed on their lives.

SELF-CONTROL

Self-control is the ability to exercise restraint and discipline over one's desires and actions. God demonstrated self-control by withholding judgment and extending mercy to His people, giving them opportunities to repent and turn back to Him. He patiently worked with them, giving them chances to change their ways. God's self-control is seen in His restrained response to human rebellion and sin. He exercises patience and gives people opportunities to repent before bringing judgment (Nehemiah 9:17).

Jesus consistently displayed self-control, particularly in resisting temptation and staying focused on His mission. In Matthew 4:1-11, Jesus was tempted by the devil in the wilderness but demonstrated self-control by not succumbing to temptation. He remained steadfast in His commitment to God's plan and purpose. Jesus demonstrated self-control when He resisted the temptation to save Himself during His crucifixion. In Matthew 27:42-43, as He hung on the cross, people taunted Him, saying,

"He saved others but he can't save himself!" Despite the temptation to prove Himself, Jesus exercised self-control, remaining focused on accomplishing the Father's will and the salvation of humanity.

Throughout the Bible we see numerous examples of how God demonstrated each fruit of the Spirit in His interactions with His people. From His love and patience with the Israelites to His faithfulness and goodness in fulfilling His promises, God consistently exhibited these qualities, showing us how we should live and relate to others. The Fruit of the Spirit serves as a model for believers to cultivate and display these virtues in their own lives. "There are in the end three things that last: Faith, Hope, and Love, and the greatest of these is Love." 1 Corinthians 13: 13.

CHAPTER 10:

GOD IS PERSONAL

God is not impressed by religious rituals. Rather, His desire is for people to seek Him, drawn near to Him, and experience a personal relationship with Him. God is a personal being, or more precisely, three personal beings, Father, Son, and Holy Spirit. In the Bible, there are several instances where God is portrayed as a personal being who relates to humanity using family terms, such as Father, Children, and Brother.

GOD AS A FATHER

In the New Testament, Jesus refers to God as Father and encourages his disciples to do the same. One notable example is found in Matthew 6:9, where Jesus teaches his disciples how to pray, saying, "Our Father in heaven, hallowed be your name." This prayer, often referred to as the Lord's Prayer, establishes a personal relationship between God and believers, with God being addressed as a loving Father.

GOD'S CHILDREN

Throughout the Bible, believers are referred to as children of God. For example: 1 John 1:12-13 states: "But to all who did receive him, who believed in his name, he gave the right to become children of God, who were born, not of blood nor of the will of the flesh nor of the will of man, but of God." In this verse, those who receive and believe in Jesus Christ are given the privilege to become children of God. This designation emphasizes the new spiritual birth believers experience when they trust in Christ.

Romans 8:14-17: "For all who are led by the Spirit of God are sons of God. For you did not receive the spirit of slavery to fall back into fear, but you have received the Spirit of adoption as sons, by whom we cry, 'Abba! Father!' The Spirit himself bears witness with our spirit that we are children of God, and if children, then heirs—heirs of God and fellow heirs with Christ, provided we suffer with him in order that we may also be glorified with him." Here, believers are described as sons (a term inclusive of both genders) of God through the Spirit of adoption. This adoption into God's family grants them a close and intimate relationship with Him and the assurance of future glory.

Galatians 3:26: "For in Christ Jesus you are all sons of God, through faith." Through faith in Jesus Christ, believers are identified as sons of God. This emphasizes the unifying aspect of our relationship with God, as all who trust in Christ share in this identity as God's children.

1 John 3:1-2: "See what kind of love the Father has given to us, that we should be called children of God; and so we are. The reason why the world does not know us is that it

did not know him. Beloved, we are God's children now, and what we will be has not yet appeared; but we know that when he appears we shall be like him because we shall see him as he is." Believers are called children of God as an expression of the Father's incredible love toward them. It signifies the present reality of their relationship with God and the future hope of being transformed into the likeness of Christ.

These passages highlight the reason believers are called children of God: through faith in Jesus Christ, they are adopted into God's family, receiving the rights and privileges of being His children. It signifies a profound and personal relationship with God as our Father, and emphasizes the love, inheritance, and future glory we have in Him.

GOD AS A BROTHER

In the New Testament, believers are described as being part of the family of God, with Jesus as their elder brother. In Hebrews 2:11, it says, "Both the one who makes people holy and those who are made holy are of the same family. So, Jesus is not ashamed to call them brothers and sisters." This verse shows the familial bond between Jesus and believers, emphasizing the intimate relationship between God and His children.

Matthew 12:50: "For whoever does the will of my Father in heaven is my brother and sister and mother." Jesus used this statement to emphasize that spiritual relationships and obedience to God's will are more significant than physical relationships.

Mark 3:35: "Whoever does God's will is my brother and sister and mother." Similar to the previous verse, Jesus highlights the importance of following God's will and how it establishes a familial bond with Him.

John 20:17: "Jesus said to her [Mary Magdalene], 'Do not cling to me, for I have not yet ascended to the Father; but go to my brothers and say to them, I am ascending to my Father and your Father, to my God and your God." After His resurrection, Jesus referred to His disciples as "brothers" to indicate the new relationship they had with God as a result of His redemptive work.

Hebrews 2:11: "For he who sanctifies and those who are sanctified all have one source. That is why he is not ashamed to call them brothers." This verse explains that Jesus, as the one who sanctifies (makes holy), and believers who are sanctified by Him share a common source, which is God the Father. Thus, Jesus is not ashamed to call them brothers.

Following are additional instances in the Bible where God is portrayed as a personal being.

GOD AS A SHEPHERD

In Psalm 23:1, King David declares, "The Lord is my shepherd; I shall not want." This metaphor portrays God as a caring and protective shepherd, guiding and providing for His people like a shepherd does for his flock. The shepherd imagery reflects a close and personal relationship between God and His followers.

GOD AS A COMFORTER

In 2 Corinthians 1:3-4, the apostle Paul writes, "Praise be to the God and Father of our Lord Jesus Christ, the Father of compassion and the God of all comfort, who comforts us in all our troubles so that we can comfort those in any trouble with the comfort we ourselves receive from God." Here, God is depicted as a compassionate Father who comforts His children in times of distress and empowers them to comfort others.

GOD AS A BRIDEGROOM

In Isaiah 62:5, it says, "As a young man marries a young woman, so will your sons marry you; as a bridegroom rejoices over his bride, so will your God rejoice over you." This imagery portrays God as a loving bridegroom who delights in His people, emphasizing the deep affection and joy God has for His chosen ones.

GOD AS A FRIEND

In John 15:15, Jesus says to His disciples, "I no longer call you servants because a servant does not know his master's business. Instead, I have called you friends, for everything that I learned from my Father I have made known to you." Jesus extends an intimate relationship with His disciples, elevating them from mere servants to trusted friends. This demonstrates God's desire for a personal connection with His followers.

GOD AS AN ADVOCATE

In 1 John 2:1, it says, "My dear children, I write this to you so that you will not sin. But if anybody does sin, we have an advocate with the Father—Jesus Christ, the Righteous One." Here, God is portrayed as an Advocate who stands on behalf of believers, showing His care and concern for their well-being.

We also see in the Bible where God makes Himself approachable to humanity in both the Old Covenant and the New Covenant. In the Old Covenant the Israelites had access to God through the Tabernacle, the Mercy Seat and the Temple.

THE TABERNACLE

In the Old Testament, God instructed Moses to build the Tabernacle, a portable sanctuary, as a place for His presence to dwell among the Israelites. Exodus 25:8 records God's command, saying, "Then have them make a sanctuary for me, and I will dwell among them." The Tabernacle served as a tangible meeting place where the Israelites could approach God and seek His presence.

THE MERCY SEAT

Within the Tabernacle, there was a special covering called the Mercy Seat, located on top of the Ark of the Covenant. In Exodus 25:22, God says, "There, above the cover between the two cherubim that are over the ark of the covenant law, I will meet with you and give you all my commands for the Israelites." The Mercy Seat symbolized God's presence and served as a place of encounter and communication between God and His people.

THE TEMPLE

Following the construction of the Tabernacle, a permanent temple was later built in Jerusalem. In 2 Chronicles 7:16, God affirms His presence in the temple, saying, "I have chosen and consecrated this temple so that my Name may be there forever. My eyes and my heart will always be there." The temple became a central place of worship where people could come to seek God's forgiveness, guidance, and presence.

In the New Covenant, which was a better covenant, we have the greatest manifestation of God's personal nature in the person of Jesus Christ.

JESUS CHRIST

The ultimate example of God's approachability and accessibility to humanity is seen in the person of Jesus Christ. In John 1:14, it says, "The Word became flesh and made his dwelling among us." Jesus, being fully God and fully human, came to Earth to bridge the gap between God and humanity. He invites people to approach Him, offering forgiveness, salvation, and a personal relationship with God.

THE HOLY SPIRIT

After Jesus' resurrection and ascension, God sent the Holy Spirit to dwell within believers. In 1 Corinthians 6:19, it says, "Do you not know that your bodies are temples of the Holy Spirit, who is in you, whom you have received from God?" The indwelling presence of the Holy Spirit allows believers to have constant access to God's presence, guidance, and empowerment.

These last two examples demonstrate how God has made Himself personal and approachable in the most intimate way possible, through a personal relationship with Jesus and the Holy Spirit. This special privilege is afforded to all born again Christians.

CHAPTER 11

GOD IS ETERNAL

Eternity is a profoundly challenging concept for us, finite beings, to fully grasp. It refers to a state of infinite or everlasting existence, transcending the boundaries of time and space as we know them. While our human minds are naturally oriented towards understanding and perceiving the world in terms of beginnings and endings, the notion of eternity surpasses those limitations, pushing the boundaries of our comprehension.

One reason why eternity is difficult to comprehend is that our everyday experiences are bound by time. We are born, we grow, we experience the passing of moments, and eventually, we come to an end. Time, shapes our understanding of life and the universe. We perceive events in terms of past, present, and future, and we measure durations through hours, days, and years. Consequently, trying to conceive of something that has no beginning or end challenges our mental abilities.

Moreover, our understanding of the physical world is grounded in the concept of cause and effect. We observe that everything has a cause, and that cause leads to an effect. We see cycles and patterns in nature, birth and decay, creation and destruction. Simple logic, however, tells us that something must be eternal. If you start with nothing, you'll end up with nothing. But we have something, so we must have started with something. In other words, since something exists now something must have always existed. There could never have been a time when absolutely nothing existed. Something must be eternal, but what is that something? The best answer to that question is God. God is eternal. He always was and He always will be. Thus, His name "I AM" is most appropriate. As we see in the Bible, the eternal nature of God is a well-established truth for those who believe in the Divine inspiration of the scriptures.

Time is a creation of God. Scripture speaks of events in the past, present and future. However, God has never been bound to time. He sees all things in the present. The Bible says: "But do not ignore this one fact, beloved, that with the Lord one day is like a thousand years, and a thousand years are like one day (2 Peter 3:8)."

The Bible also says that God inhabits eternity. "For thus says the high and lofty one who inhabits eternity, whose name is Holy: I dwell in the high and holy place, and also with those who are contrite and humble in spirit, to revive the spirit of the humble, and to revive the heart of the contrite." (Isaiah 57:15).

The doctrine of the eternity of God provides comfort to believers. Since God will never cease to exist neither will those who have put their trust in Him. Jesus says, "Whoever hears my word and believes him who sent me has eternal life. He does not come into judgment but has passed from death to life." (John 5:24).

Following are some additional scriptures that speak to the eternal nature of God:

Psalm 102:25-27: Speaks of the eternal nature of God and His creative power. It emphasizes that God is the Creator who laid the foundations of the earth and established the heavens. The passage asserts that while the earth and heavens will perish, God will remain unchanged and endure forever. This psalm reminds us of God's sovereignty and His everlasting nature. "Of old you laid the foundation of the earth, and the heavens are the work of your hands. They will perish, but you will remain; they will all wear out like a garment. You will change them like a robe, and they will pass away, but you are the same, and your years have no end."

Exodus 3:14: In Exodus 3:14, Moses encounters God in the form of a burning bush and asks Him what name he should use to refer to Him when delivering the Israelites from Egypt. God responds by saying, "I am who I am" or "I will be what I will be." This divine self-identification highlights God's self-existence and eternal nature. It signifies that God is the unchanging and self-sufficient Being, existing independently of anything else. It demonstrates God's authority and sovereignty over all things.

Micah 5:2: Prophesies the birth of the Messiah in Bethlehem, the city of David. The verse states, "But you, Bethlehem Ephrathah, though you are small among the clans of Judah, out of you will come for me one who will be ruler over Israel, whose origins are from of old, from ancient times." This prophecy is fulfilled in the New Testament when Jesus, the Messiah, is born in Bethlehem. It emphasizes the preexistence of the Messiah, highlighting His eternal origins and His divine nature.

Hebrews 1:10-12: these verses quote from Psalm 102:25-27, applying it to Jesus Christ. The passage portrays Jesus as the Son of God who laid the foundations of the earth and will outlast the created order. It affirms the deity and eternality of Jesus, declaring His superiority over angels and all creation. By quoting this psalm, the author of Hebrews underscores Jesus' divine nature, His role as the Creator, and His unchanging existence.

John 1:1-2: Is the opening passage of the Gospel of John, describing the divine nature of Jesus Christ. It states, "In the beginning was the Word, and the Word was with God, and the Word was God. He was with God in the beginning." Here, the "Word" refers to Jesus Christ. This passage highlights the eternal existence of Jesus and His identity as both distinct from and united with God the Father. It affirms the deity of Jesus, emphasizing that He was present with God from the beginning and played a central role in creation. This verse lays the foundation for the Gospel of John's portrayal of Jesus as the Son of God and the incarnate Word.

Psalm 90:2. "Before the mountains were born or you brought forth the whole world, from everlasting to everlasting you are God." This verse acknowledges the timeless nature of God, emphasizing that He has existed before the creation of the world and will continue to exist forever. It highlights the eternal nature of God's being and establishes Him as the unchanging foundation of all existence.

Psalm 93:2. "Your throne, O Lord, has stood from time immemorial. You yourself are from the everlasting past." This verse portrays God's throne as an eternal and unshakable seat of authority. It affirms that God's rule extends beyond the bounds of time and emphasizes His eternal reign as the sovereign Lord of all creation.

Isaiah 40:28 "Do you not know? Have you not heard? The Lord is the everlasting God, the Creator of the ends of the earth. He will not grow tired or weary, and his understanding no one can fathom." This verse emphasizes the incomparable nature of God's eternal existence. It affirms that God, as the everlasting Creator, possesses limitless energy and understanding. It assures us that God is unwavering and inexhaustible in His care for His creation.

Isaiah 57:15 "The high and lofty one who lives in eternity, the Holy One, says this: I live in the high and holy place with those whose spirits are contrite and humble. I restore the crushed spirit of the humble and revive the courage of those with repentant hearts." This verse describes God as the exalted and holy One who dwells in eternity. It reveals His willingness to be intimately present with those who approach Him with humility and contrition. It assures us that God's eternal nature encompasses His redemptive work of restoring and uplifting the brokenhearted and contrite.

1 Timothy 1:17. "To the King of the ages, immortal, invisible, the only God, be honor and glory forever and ever. Amen." This verse acknowledges the eternal and divine attributes of God. It recognizes Him as the everlasting King, beyond human limitations of mortality and visibility. It invites the proclamation of honor and glory to God, affirming His eternal majesty.

Revelation 1:8 "I am the Alpha and the Omega, says the Lord God, who is, and who was, and who is to come, the Almighty." This verse presents God as the beginning and the end. It emphasizes His eternal existence, spanning from the past to the present and the future. It establishes God as the Almighty, affirming His eternal sovereignty and power.

Revelation 22:13. "I am the Alpha and the Omega, the First and the Last, the Beginning and the End." This verse echoes the previous verse in Revelation, reiterating that God encompasses the entirety of existence. As the Alpha and the Omega, the First and the Last, He is the eternal source and the ultimate destination. He is the eternal God who holds all things in His hands.

Deuteronomy 33:27. "The eternal God is your refuge, and underneath are the everlasting arms. He will drive out your enemies before you, saying, Destroy them!" This verse portrays God as the eternal and unchanging refuge for His people. It symbolizes His protective presence, represented by His everlasting arms.

CHAPTER 12:

GOD IS FAITHFUL

God is always faithful, and we are called to walk by faith and not by sight (2 Corinthians 5:7)

We see in the Bible (Philippians 4:19) "And my God will meet all your needs according to the riches of His glory in Christ Jesus." This verse assures us that we can trust God to provide our needs even when we don't see immediate answers to our prayers. We may not have everything we want, but we will have everything we need.

We see God's faithfulness under both the Old Covenant as well as the New Covenant. In the Old Testament, there are numerous instances where the faithfulness of God is clearly demonstrated through His responses to prayers, fulfillment of prophecies, and the delivery on promises made to His people.

ANSWERED PRAYERS

The story of Hannah in 1 Samuel 1:9-20 portrays how God answered her prayer for a child. Despite years of barrenness, Hannah fervently prayed to God, and He blessed her with a son, Samuel, who later became a great prophet and leader in Israel.

In the book of Daniel, chapter 9, Daniel prays for the restoration of Jerusalem and the forgiveness of the people's sins. God hears Daniel's prayer and sends the angel Gabriel to provide him with a vision and understanding.

FULFILLED PROPHECIES

The prophecy of the Messiah in the Old Testament finds its fulfillment in Jesus Christ. Numerous prophecies in books like Isaiah (e.g., Isaiah 7:14, 9:6-7) and Micah (Micah 5:2) foretold the birth, life, death, and resurrection of Jesus, which were ultimately fulfilled in the New Testament.

The prophecy regarding the exile and restoration of the Israelites is another example. In Jeremiah 29:10, God assures the Israelites that after seventy years of Babylonian captivity, He would bring them back to their homeland. This prophecy came to pass when Cyrus, the king of Persia, issued a decree allowing the Israelites to return and rebuild Jerusalem.

DELIVERY ON PROMISES

God's promise to Abraham in Genesis 12:1-3 illustrates His faithfulness. He promised to make Abraham a great nation and bless all the families of the earth through him. Despite Abraham's doubts and the challenges, he faced, God remained faithful to His promise, and Abraham became the father of the nation of Israel.

The promise of the land of Canaan to the Israelites is another significant example. In Exodus 3:17, God assures Moses that He will bring the Israelites out of Egypt and into a land flowing with milk and honey. Eventually, after wandering in the wilderness for forty years, God fulfills His promise and leads them into the Promised Land under the leadership of Joshua.

These instances and many others throughout the Old Testament demonstrate God's faithfulness in answering prayers, fulfilling prophecies, and delivering on promises. They reveal His unwavering commitment to His people and his trustworthy nature as a God who keeps His word.

Deuteronomy 7:9: "Know therefore that the LORD your God is God, the faithful God who keeps covenant and steadfast love with those who love him and keep his commandments, to a thousand generations." This verse emphasizes that God is faithful, and His faithfulness extends for generations, showing His enduring commitment to His people.

Psalm 36:5: "Your steadfast love, O LORD, extends to the heavens, your faithfulness to the clouds." This verse praises God's faithfulness, and portrays His unwavering love and reliability.

Lamentations 3:22-23: "The steadfast love of the LORD never ceases; his mercies never come to an end; they are new every morning; great is your faithfulness." These verses express the unfailing faithfulness of God. Despite difficult circumstances, His steadfast love and mercies never come to an end. His faithfulness is constant and renewed each day.

Isaiah 25:1: "O LORD, you are my God; I will exalt you; I will praise your name, for you have done wonderful things, plans formed of old, faithful and sure." This verse acknowledges God's faithfulness and sureness in fulfilling His plans. It highlights His reliability and trustworthiness in carrying out His purposes.

Psalm 89:8: "O LORD God of hosts, who is mighty as you are, O LORD, with your faithfulness all around you?" This verse recognizes the faithfulness of God as encompassing His entire being. It emphasizes His power and reliability, affirming that His faithfulness is present in every aspect of His nature.

Psalm 119:90: "Your faithfulness endures to all generations; you have established the earth, and it stands fast." This verse emphasizes the enduring nature of God's faithfulness. It declares that His faithfulness extends to all generations, highlighting His unwavering commitment throughout time.

Nehemiah 9:31: "Nevertheless, in your great mercies, you did not make an end of them or forsake them, for you are a gracious and merciful God." This verse reflects on God's great mercy and faithfulness. It acknowledges that despite the people's shortcomings, God did not forsake them. His faithfulness is demonstrated through His graciousness and compassion

2 Samuel 7:28: "And now, O Lord GOD, you are God, and your words are true, and you have promised this good thing to your servant." This verse praises God's faithfulness in fulfilling His promises. It acknowledges the truthfulness of God's words and expresses gratitude for His faithfulness in bringing about good things.

Joshua 23:14: "And now I am about to go the way of all the earth, and you know in your hearts and souls, all of you, that not one word has failed of all the good things that the LORD your God promised concerning you. All have come to pass for you; not one of them has failed." This verse testifies to God's faithfulness in keeping His promises. It affirms that every word spoken by the Lord has come to pass and not one has failed. It highlights God's trustworthiness and reliability in fulfilling His commitments.

These verses emphasize God's faithfulness as a consistent theme throughout the Old Testament, reaffirming His trustworthiness, steadfast love, and commitment to His people and His promises.

Under the New Covenant, there are several instances that highlight the faithfulness of God.

Answered Prayer

In the Gospel of Luke, we see the story of Zechariah and Elizabeth, an elderly couple who had been unable to conceive a child. Zechariah, while serving as a priest in the temple, had an encounter with an angel who told him that his wife would bear a son named John, who would prepare the way for the Lord. Despite initially doubting the angel's words, Zechariah's prayer for a child was eventually answered, and Elizabeth gave birth to John the Baptist, fulfilling God's promise (Luke 1:5-25).

Matthew 7:7-8: "Ask, and it will be given to you; seek, and you will find; knock, and it will be opened to you. For everyone who asks receives, and the one who seeks finds, and to the one who knocks it will be opened." These verses emphasize the assurance that God answers prayers when approached with faith and persistence.

John 14:13-14: "Whatever you ask in my name, this I will do, that the Father may be glorified in the Son. If you ask me anything in my name, I will do it." Jesus promises that when we pray in His name, according to His will, He will answer our prayers, ultimately bringing glory to God.

FULFILLED PROPHECIES

Throughout the New Testament, we find numerous prophecies from the Old Testament fulfilled in the life, death, and resurrection of Jesus Christ. For example, the prophet Isaiah foretold that a virgin would conceive and bear a son, and he would be called Immanuel, which means "God with us" (Isaiah 7:14).

Matthew 1:22-23: "All this took place to fulfill what the Lord had spoken by the prophet: 'Behold, the virgin shall conceive and bear a son, and they shall call his name Immanuel' (which means, God with us)." This verse highlights the fulfillment of Isaiah's prophecy regarding the birth of Jesus, proving God's faithfulness in fulfilling His promises.

Acts 2:16-21: In this passage, the apostle Peter quotes the prophecy of Joel, saying, "And in the last days it shall be, God declares, that I will pour out my Spirit on all flesh." Peter affirms that the outpouring of the Holy Spirit on the day of Pentecost fulfills Joel's prophecy, illustrating God's faithfulness in fulfilling His word.

FULFILLED PROMISES

One of the central themes in the New Testament is the fulfillment of God's promises through Jesus Christ. In the book of Acts, the apostle Peter addresses a crowd and declares that the outpouring of the Holy Spirit upon the believers was a fulfillment of God's promise spoken through the prophet Joel (Acts 2:16-21). The promise of salvation through faith in Jesus Christ, eternal life, and the indwelling of the Holy Spirit are among the many promises fulfilled in the New Testament.

2 Corinthians 1:20: "For all the promises of God find their Yes in him. That is why it is through him that we utter our Amen to God for his glory." This verse reassures believers that all of God's promises are fulfilled in Christ, reinforcing His faithfulness to fulfill what He has spoken.

Hebrews 10:23: "Let us hold fast the confession of our hope without wavering, for he who promised is faithful." This verse encourages believers to remain steadfast in their faith, knowing that the One who made the promises is faithful and will fulfill them.

These verses provide a glimpse into the New Testament's affirmation of God's faithfulness in answering prayers, fulfilling prophecies, and keeping His promises. They demonstrate the trustworthiness of God and His commitment to fulfill His Word. These examples demonstrate that God is reliable and trustworthy, faithfully working throughout history to bring about His plans and purposes.

CHAPTER 13:

GOD IS UNCHANGING

These two Bible verses say it all, Malachi 3:6 and Hebrews 13:8.

Malachi 3: 6 says: "Surely, I the Lord do not change When we consider that God was always perfect, He cannot change without compromising His perfection. If some change in His being brings improvement, then He was at some point incomplete and therefore not perfect. If a change in His being was a negative change, then He is now imperfect. Can't happen!

Hebrews 13:8 is a powerful and significant verse that holds deep meaning for Christians. It states, "Jesus Christ is the same yesterday and today and forever." This verse highlights the eternal and unchanging nature of Jesus Christ, emphasizing His consistency, reliability, and everlasting presence.

The author of Hebrews, in this verse, affirms the enduring nature of Jesus Christ. By stating that He is the same "yesterday, today, and forever," it underscores the timeless and unchangeable character of Jesus. This attribute is crucial for believers because it assures them that Jesus' love, faithfulness, and teachings remain constant across all ages. It affirms the unshakable foundation of the

Christian faith, built upon the unchanging nature of the Son of God.

Moreover, this verse encourages believers to put their trust in Jesus Christ. In a world that is constantly changing and filled with uncertainties, this verse provides solace and hope. It reminds Christians that amidst the ever-shifting circumstances of life, Jesus remains steadfast and unwavering. He is the anchor that believers can rely on, providing stability and guidance in every season.

The verse also has practical implications for how Christians should live their lives. Since Jesus Christ remains the same, His teachings and principles continue to be relevant and applicable today. It encourages believers to follow His example, imitating His love, compassion, and righteousness. It serves as a reminder that the truths and values found in the teachings of Jesus are timeless and provide a solid foundation for a godly life.

Overall, Hebrews 13:8 is a verse that encapsulates the unchanging nature of Jesus Christ and encourages believers to find comfort, guidance, and assurance in Him. It reminds Christians of the enduring power and relevance of the Gospel, urging them to place their faith and trust in the eternal Son of God.

Changes in life are a constant for us. The advancements of modern science may tell us that a person's DNA code remains the same throughout his life, but we all know that we change physically, mentally, morally, and spiritually over time. However, as the above passage tells us, while creatures necessarily change, such change does not apply to the Creator.

The Lord is immutable; it is impossible for His character or being to undergo any mutation. His power cannot be augmented or diminished. He never learns or forgets, and He cannot be anything other than perfectly holy. Human beings can change in a multitude of ways, but our God remains ever the same.

God's immutability does not mean that He cannot move or that He remains inert. In fact, Scripture in many places testifies of the Lord's constant work to sustain creation. For example, Hebrews 1: 3a says, This Son is a reflection of the Father's glory, the exact representation of the Father's being and He sustains all things by His powerful word." His unchanging love led Him to free His people from Egyptian slavery. Exodus 2: 23-25.

Furthermore, the Lord's unchanging character does not mean His relationship with us is not real. Jonathan Edwards said immutability provokes sinners to enmity. Many in the world hate God because they know that His unchangeableness guarantees He cannot forget or overlook their rebellion. It is His unchanging righteousness that results in His wrath toward the impenitent as we see in Romans 1: 18-32:

"The wrath of God is being revealed from heaven against all the godlessness and wickedness of people, who suppress the truth by their wickedness, since what may be known about God is plain to them, because God has made it plain to them. For since the creation of the world God's invisible qualities—his eternal power and divine nature—have been clearly seen, being understood from what has been made, so that people are without excuse.

For although they knew God, they neither glorified him as God nor gave thanks to him, but their thinking became futile and their foolish hearts were darkened. Although they claimed to be wise, they became fools and exchanged the glory of the immortal God for images made to look like a mortal human being and birds and animals and reptiles.

Therefore, God gave them over in the sinful desires of their hearts to sexual impurity for the degrading of their bodies with one another. They exchanged the truth about God for a lie, and worshiped and served created things rather than the Creator—who is forever praised. Amen.

Because of this, God gave them over to shameful lusts. Even their women exchanged natural sexual relations for unnatural ones. In the same way the men also abandoned natural relations with women and were inflamed with lust for one another. Men committed shameful acts with other men, and received in themselves the due penalty for their error.

Furthermore, just as they did not think it worthwhile to retain the knowledge of God, so God gave them over to a depraved mind, so that they do what ought not to be done. They have become filled with every kind of wickedness, evil, greed and depravity. They are full of envy, murder, strife, deceit, and malice. They are gossips, slanderers, God-haters, insolent, arrogant and boastful; they invent ways of doing evil; they disobey their parents; they have no understanding, no fidelity, no love, no mercy. Although they know God's righteous decree that those who do such things deserve death, they not only continue to do these very things but also approve of those who practice them."

Several additional Bible verses show that God never changes:

Numbers 23:19: "God is not human, that he should lie, not a human being, that he should change his mind. Does he speak and then not act? Does he promise and not fulfill?" This verse emphasizes the unchanging nature of God. It highlights the fact that God is faithful and reliable, always fulfilling His promises. It reminds us that we can trust in His word and rely on His faithfulness.

Isaiah 40:8: "The grass withers and the flowers fall, but the word of our God endures forever." This verse emphasizes the eternal nature and lasting power of God's word. It contrasts the temporary nature of earthly things with the everlasting truth of God's word. It reminds us that God's word is a firm foundation that remains constant and reliable throughout time.

Psalm 102:25-27: "In the beginning you laid the foundations of the earth, and the heavens are the work of your hands. They will perish, but you remain; they will all wear out like a garment. Like clothing, you will change them and they will be discarded. But you remain the same, and your years will never end." These verses speak of God's eternal nature and His creative power. They acknowledge the changing nature of creation, which will eventually wear out, but God Himself remains unchanged and eternal.

Matthew 24:35: "Heaven and earth will pass away, but my words will never pass away." This verse emphasizes the enduring authority and reliability of Jesus' words. It highlights the contrast between the temporary nature of the world and the everlasting truth of His teachings. It reassures believers that Jesus' words are timeless and will always hold their power and significance.

Isaiah 40:28: "Do you not know? Have you not heard? The LORD is the everlasting God, the Creator of the ends of the earth. He will not grow tired or weary, and his understanding no one can fathom." This verse underscores the incomparable nature of God's strength and wisdom. It reassures us that God is eternal and unchanging, and His understanding is beyond human comprehension. It reminds us that we can find strength and comfort in the everlasting nature of God.

Psalm 46:10: "Be still, and know that I am God; I will be exalted among the nations, I will be exalted in the earth." This verse encourages us to trust in God's sovereignty and power. It calls us to find rest and peace in recognizing His authority over all things. It reminds us that God will ultimately be exalted and glorified in the world.

Psalm 90:2: "Before the mountains were born or you brought forth the whole world, from everlasting to everlasting you are God." This verse emphasizes God's eternal existence and His position as the Creator of all things. It highlights the fact that God has always existed and will continue to exist for all eternity.

Isaiah 44:6: "This is what the LORD says—Israel's King and Redeemer, the LORD Almighty: I am the first and I am the last; apart from me there is no God." This verse declares God's unique position as the one and only God. It emphasizes His sovereignty and authority over all creation. It reminds us that there is no other deity besides Him.

Revelation 22:13: "I am the Alpha and the Omega, the First and the Last, the Beginning and the End." This verse echoes the sentiment of

Isaiah 44:6, emphasizing God's eternal nature and His supremacy over all things. It highlights that God is the ultimate source and destination of all existence. It assures us that God's reign is absolute and eternal.

CHAPTER 14:

GOD IS OMNIPRESENT

God's omnipresence refers to His attribute of being present everywhere at the same time. It means that God is not limited by time, space, or physical boundaries. His presence extends over the entire universe, encompassing every place and every moment simultaneously.

GOD'S TRANSCENDENCE AND IMMANENCE

God's omnipresence is related to His transcendence and immanence. Transcendence emphasizes that God is above and beyond His creation, existing outside of it. Immanence highlights that God is intimately involved and present within His creation. God's omnipresence encompasses both aspects, as He is not limited or confined by His creation, yet He is actively present within it.

UNRESTRICTED PRESENCE

God's omnipresence means that there is no place where God is absent. He fills all space, both visible and invisible. Whether in the highest heavens or the deepest depths, God is fully present. This unrestricted presence brings comfort, as it means that believers can never be separated from God's presence.

PERSONAL AND UNIVERSAL PRESENCE

God's omnipresence is both personal and universal. Personally, God is intimately present with each individual believer. He knows them deeply and is near to them in every circumstance. Universally, God's presence extends over the entire cosmos, sustaining and upholding all things.

ACTIVE INVOLVEMENT

God's omnipresence is not a passive presence but an active one. He is not merely observing from a distance but is actively involved in every aspect of His creation. God's presence brings guidance, protection, provision, and comfort. He is present to hear prayers, to answer, and to interact with His creation.

SIMULTANEOUS PRESENCE

God's omnipresence allows Him to be fully present in multiple locations and situations simultaneously. He is not divided or diminished in His presence. God's infinite nature enables Him to be fully present with every individual, every community, and every moment in time.

Recognizing and embracing God's omnipresence can deepen our relationship with Him. It reminds us that we are never alone, that He is always accessible, and that we can approach Him at any time and in any place. It also encourages reverence and awe, acknowledging that we stand in the presence of the Almighty.

"I Am"

FOLLOWING ARE SCRIPTURES THAT
SPEAK TO GOD'S OMNIPRESENCE

Psalm 139:7-10: "Where can I go from your Spirit? Where can I flee from your presence? If I go up to the heavens, you are there; if I make my bed in the depths, you are there. If I rise on the wings of the dawn, if I settle on the far side of the sea, even there your hand will guide me, your right hand will hold me fast."

This psalm highlights the all-encompassing presence of God. It emphasizes that no matter where we are or what circumstances we find ourselves in, God is always with us, guiding and holding us securely.

Jeremiah 23:23-24: "Am I only a God nearby, declares the LORD, and not a God far away? Who can hide in secret places so that I cannot see them? declares the LORD. Do not I fill heaven and earth? declares the LORD."

This passage emphasizes God's omnipresence, stating that He is not limited by proximity. God is both near to us and far away, and there is no hiding from His sight. He fills the entirety of heaven and earth, underscoring His all-pervasive presence.

Acts 17:27-28: "God did this so that they would seek him and perhaps reach out for him and find him, though he is not far from any one of us. For in him we live and move and have our being. As some of your own poets have said, we are his offspring."

This verse highlights that God is not far from any individual. It asserts that in God, we live, move, and have our being. Our existence and connection to Him are inseparable, emphasizing His omnipresence in sustaining and upholding our lives.

Proverbs 15:3: "The eyes of the LORD are everywhere, keeping watch on the wicked and the good."

This concise proverb conveys the idea that God's eyes are ever-present, observing everything that happens. His watchful gaze extends over both the wicked and the righteous, indicating His awareness and involvement in all aspects of human affairs.

Matthew 28:20: "...And surely I am with you always, to the very end of the age."

Jesus spoke these words to His disciples before ascending to heaven. He assured them that He would be with them always, indicating His divine presence through the Holy Spirit. This promise extends to all believers, emphasizing God's perpetual presence in their lives.

1 Kings 8:27: "But will God really dwell on earth? The heavens, even the highest heaven, cannot contain you. How much less this temple I have built!"

This verse, spoken by Solomon during the dedication of the temple, acknowledges the vastness of God's presence. It recognizes that even the grandest physical structure cannot contain Him, emphasizing His omnipresence.

Isaiah 66:1: "This is what the LORD says: Heaven is my throne, and the earth is my footstool. Where is the house you will build for me? Where will my resting place be?"

In this passage, God declares that the entire universe is under His dominion. Heaven is His throne, and the earth is merely His footstool. It conveys His omnipresence by indicating that no human structure can confine or encompass His presence.

Matthew 18:20: "For where two or three gather in my name, there am I with them."

Jesus assures His followers that whenever they gather in His name, He is present among them. This verse emphasizes His omnipresence in the context of communal worship and fellowship, promising His presence whenever believers unite.

Ephesians 4:6: "One God and Father of all, who is over all and through all and in all."

This verse emphasizes the all-encompassing presence of God. It states that He is overall, through all, and in all, highlighting His omnipresence and His active involvement in every aspect of creation.

Understanding and contemplating God's omnipresence can bring comfort, assurance, and a sense of awe. It reminds us that God is not distant or disconnected but is actively present in our lives, sustaining, guiding, and loving us at all times and in all places.

CHAPTER 15:

GOD IS SPIRIT

The concept that "God is Spirit" is derived from various biblical passages that describe the nature of God. One of the key verses often referenced is found in the Gospel of John, where Jesus says, "God is spirit, and his worshipers must worship in the Spirit and in truth" (John 4:24).

When we say that "God is Spirit," we mean that God's essence or nature is spiritual rather than physical. Unlike human beings or any created thing, God does not have a physical body or exist within the confines of time and space. God is immaterial and transcendent, existing beyond the material world.

The concept of God as Spirit implies several important attributes:

1. Immateriality: God is not composed of physical matter. He is not limited by the material constraints that govern the created universe.

2. Transcendence: God exists beyond the boundaries of the physical universe. He is not confined to a particular location or restricted by the laws of nature.

3. Omnipresence: Since God is Spirit, He is present everywhere. His presence is not limited to a specific

physical location but extends throughout the entirety of creation.

4. Invisibility: Because God is Spirit, He cannot be seen with physical eyes. His true nature is hidden from our physical perception.

5. Personal and relational: While God is Spirit, He is also a personal being who desires to have a relationship with His creation. Though we cannot perceive God's Spirit with our physical senses, we can experience His presence through our spirits and through His interactions with us.

The following scriptures speak to God as Spirit:

John 4:24: "God is spirit, and his worshipers must worship in the Spirit and in truth."

This verse is often cited as the clearest statement in the Bible affirming that God is Spirit. It emphasizes the importance of worshiping God not merely in external rituals but with an authentic and genuine spirit.

2 Corinthians 3:17: "Now the Lord is the Spirit, and where the Spirit of the Lord is, there is freedom."

This verse highlights the connection between the Lord (referring to Jesus) and the Holy Spirit. It suggests the presence of the Spirit brings freedom and liberation.

John 3:6: "Flesh gives birth to flesh, but the Spirit gives birth to spirit."

In this verse, Jesus speaks about the contrast between physical birth (flesh) and spiritual birth (Spirit). It implies that God, as Spirit, is the source of spiritual life and transformation.

Romans 8:9: "You, however, are not in the realm of the flesh but are in the realm of the Spirit if indeed the Spirit of God lives in you. And if anyone does not have the Spirit of Christ, they do not belong to Christ."

This verse emphasizes the distinction between living according to the flesh and living according to the Spirit. It suggests that having the Spirit of God dwelling within a person is a defining characteristic of being a follower of Christ.

1 Corinthians 2:11: "For who knows a person's thoughts except their own spirit within them? In the same way no one knows the thoughts of God except the Spirit of God."

This verse draws a parallel between a person's inner spirit and the Spirit of God. It highlights the idea that the Spirit of God is intimately connected with God's thoughts and intentions.

John 6:63: "The Spirit gives life; the flesh counts for nothing. The words I have spoken to you—they are full of the Spirit and life."

Jesus speaks these words, emphasizing the life-giving power of the Spirit. It suggests that the Spirit brings spiritual vitality and understanding, while physical matters are of lesser significance.

These scriptures provide a glimpse into the biblical affirmation that God is Spirit. They highlight the spiritual nature of God, the relationship between God and the Holy Spirit, and the role of the Spirit in human life and worship.

In Chapter 2 of this book, "God is Almighty," we listed some of the works of the Holy Spirit. It is worth repeating these as they would not be possible if God were not Spirit.

Listed here with the Biblical references are some of the things He is doing for the believers.

- In Romans 8:26 Holy Spirit helps us pray and He intercedes for us

- In John 16:13 He guides us into all truth and announces to us things to come.

- In John 14:26 He instructs us in everything and reminds of what Jesus taught us.

- In Revelation 2:7. He speaks to the Church.

- In 1 Corinthians 2:10 He reveals wisdom to us.

- In Acts 9:31 He builds up and consoles the Church.

- In Acts 1:8 and 4:31 He fills us and empowers us by the Baptism in the Holy Spirit.

- In 1 Corinthians 12:8-10 He gives us supernatural gifts.

- In Ephesians 3:16 He strengthens us.

- In 2 Peter 1:21 He Prophesies through us.

- In 1 Thessalonians 1:6 He gives us joy despite great trials.

- In 2 Corinthians 3:17 He gives us freedom.

- In Revelations 22:17 He calls for the return of Jesus.

- In 2 Corinthians 3:18 He transform us into the image of Jesus.

- In 1 Corinthians 3:16 He lives in us making us a temple of God.

- In Romans 8:2 He frees us from the law of sin and death.

- In Galatians 12:8-10 He produces fruit (good character traits) in us.

- In Romans 8:14 He leads us in life.

- In Romans 8:16 He testifies that we are children of God.

- In Ephesians 4:3 He unites us in the Body of Christ.

- In Ephesians 1:13 He seals us as a pledge to our inheritance.

- Matthew 12:28 He enables us to cast our demons.

In summary we can say that God is Spirit for the Holy Spirit is Spirit, and the Holy Spirit is God. The unique unity between the Father, the Son, and the Holy Spirit is such that they share equally in all the Divine attributes, including the Spirit nature.

Finally, the Word of God tells us that He is a rewarder of those who diligently seek Him. If you have not done that yet, you can do it now. Jesus said, "I am the way, the truth, and the life. No one comes to the Father except through me." Ask Jesus to become your Lord and Savior, and to forgive your sins, and He will. See you in Paradise!

Printed in the USA
CPSIA information can be obtained
at www.ICGtesting.com
JSHW010528020923
47675JS00010B/386